GATHERING THE PEOPLE OF GOD

Renew the Liturgy - Renew the Church

Frank O'Loughlin

Published in Australia by
Coventry Press
33 Scoresby Road
Bayswater VIC 3153

ISBN 9780648861263

Copyright © Frank O'Loughlin 2020

All rights reserved. Other than for the purposes and subject to the conditions prescribed under the *Copyright Act*, no part of this publication may be reproduced, stored in a retrieval system, or transmitted in any form or by any means, electronic, mechanical, photocopying, recording or otherwise, without the prior permission of the publisher.

Scripture quotations are from *The Jerusalem Bible* © 1966 by Darton Longman and Todd Ltd and Doubleday and Company Ltd.

Catalogue-in-Publication entry is available from the
National Library of Australia http://catologue.nla.gov.au

Cover design by Ian James – www.jgd.com.au
Text design by Coventry Press
Set in Pagella 11.5 pt

Printed in Australia

Contents

Introduction
Renew the Liturgy,
Renew the Church 3

Chapter 1   The Church in Transition 7

Chapter 2   The Liturgy is Celebrated in Signs 24

Chapter 3   The Work of the
            People of God 39

Chapter 4   The Sunday Eucharist 48

Chapter 5   Liturgical Prayer 57

Chapter 6   Already but not yet 69

Chapter 7   Numbers at Mass 76

Chapter 8   The Paschal Mystery 84

Chapter 9   The Eucharist is Pentecost 91

Chapter 10 'For you and for all' 99

Conclusion 114

*To the people
of Sacred Heart Parish Sandringham
with thanks and deep affection*

Introduction
Renew the Liturgy, Renew the Church

WHEN PEOPLE SPEAK of distancing themselves from the Church, they often say 'I don't go to Mass anymore'. There is a profound – even if not explicit – link in such a statement between the Mass and the Church. The statement implies that not being at Mass is the equivalent of not being part of the Church.

This simple statement expresses something of considerable importance. Several times throughout this book, I will refer to an adage that comes from the early centuries of Christianity. The adage states 'The Eucharist makes the Church and the Church makes the Eucharist'.

To take such a statement seriously not only makes it important that people go to Mass but also that Mass be celebrated in such a way that it does draw people into it, that it does make the Church, the gathered People of God, flourish.

Looking to this issue means that we have to take seriously the mentality behind the celebration. What is the mentality that shapes our approach to the Mass? There will be an insistence throughout this book on the theological and liturgical approach to the liturgy which arises out of the Second Vatican Council because this approach involves not just a change of texts and details of ritual but a new mindset within which to celebrate the Mass and the rest of the liturgy.

An earlier approach tended to be shaped by a legal mentality which had a disabling effect on the very nature of liturgy. It tended to thwart the deeper Christological, ecclesial and spiritual character of the liturgy. In so doing, it placed limits on the liturgy's capacity to be properly and appropriately fruitful. This brought about a type of liturgical celebration in which the people prayed during the liturgy rather than praying the liturgy itself which is the source of the true Christian spirit.

The liturgy is a celebration of the covenant. The notion of the covenant has deep roots in the whole biblical tradition: there was the covenant of the first testament made through Moses and then there is the new and eternal covenant created in the death and resurrection of Jesus. The liturgy is the exercising of that covenant; that is, it is the means by which the People of God enter into and celebrate their relationship with God in Christ. The liturgy is not just about what God does but what goes on between God and human beings in and through Jesus Christ. The liturgy is not the whole life of the Church but it is indeed the source and summit of that life.

So to renew and reform the liturgy – that is to bring it to be more fully what it is intended to be – is to renew the Church, that is to make the Church more fully what it is intended to be.

The Church, the People of God, is engaged upon this project. It is a project that touches the whole People of God, every level of the Church's life and every ministry in the Church, especially the ordained ministries.

In the new pluralist and quite secular era in which we living, our liturgy needs to manifest who we are – a People who belong to Jesus Christ, a People who belong together, a People who are to be a lantern for the one who is the light that has come into the world (John 1:9).

Chapter 1

The Church in Transition

THE CHURCH IS IN TRANSIT from one way of being the Church to another! In all the dimensions of the life of the Church, it is moving into a new era. The watershed of this transition was the Second Vatican Council of more than fifty years ago. That Council set the Church on a new path, a path upon which it continues, even though at times hesitatingly; but a path whose direction is shaping even those who do not want to take that path. We all know that there have been varied reactions to this transition but in fact all members of the Church are engaged upon it. There are those who are keen to continue on this path; those who are dubious or fearful about it; those who barely know that they are on it, those who have barely heard of the Council; and those who are refusing to take its path. But we are all being shaped by the transition that is afoot. This is true even of those who so refuse to accept the Council that they are seeking to create their own Church.

As part of this transition, there have indeed been severings with the past, particularly with the past immediately preceding the Second Vatican Council; these severings have been more painful for some than for others.

It has also become clear just how conditioned the Catholic Church has been in the period from the Council of Trent (1545-1563) to the twentieth century by the differences and conflicts between Catholicism and the Churches issuing from the Reformation. This conflict affected both the practice of the Church and its thinking. It produced its own historically conditioned form of Catholicism.

So much has been discovered about the Christian past and the many historical contexts within which the Catholic faith had been lived. These many contexts were different to that of the period following the Council of Trent and indeed different from our own contemporary context. We have also come to see and acknowledge that there had grown up in the life of the Church ideas and practices which were questionable and some that were unworthy of the gospel of Christ.

Transitions have always been part of the Church's life as they are of all human life. They can occur in greater and less intensity. The one we are living through at the moment is indeed of great intensity and importance.

Taking seriously that we must always see things in their context means that we must also be aware of our own contemporary context with the advantages and limitations that it brings about in us. We need always to be open to 'learning on the job'.

Transitions

Transitions are a part of all human life and of every human society. There are personal transitions such as adolescence, entering into a marriage relationship, taking up a profession and moving to retirement. In all of these, there is a movement into the future – which is not quite known – and there is the need to leave behind a stage of life with which we were comfortable and within which we had a sense of our identity and our place in society.

Every transition brings about a period of uncertainty that can arouse sufficient fear in us that we want to retreat into the comfortable past. There are adults who have not grown up, those who never manage to move into the shared relationship of marriage, those who cannot manage the demands of new way of life or those who cannot retire. In all these situations, people experience the desire to move forward and the desire to retreat into the past. Are not adolescents sometimes like adults and at other times like children? In all such transitions a resolution has to come about – a resolution to gather up one's courage and strength and to move ahead.

The same pattern emerges when we talk about large-scale, social transitions. There can be a clinging to a past with which we identified easily as there can be an angry reaction to a future which creates fear and disturbs our sense of identity. We can see examples of this in societies in which there is large-scale immigration. In such societies, the fear of people who are different disturbs the existing population who see their way of life and identity threatened. Similarly, we can see it in reactions to the greater participation of women in society in which some men see their role and identity being threatened.

It is in transitions that we come to discover who we really are. In the movement from one stage to another, we discover our continuing identity and leave behind things that seemed important in the earlier stage. Is this not true of adolescence? Do we not leave childhood behind as we enter gradually into adulthood and yet we are still ourselves? Is it not similar when people retire from work? Is there not a process afoot in that transition in which we discover who we are, apart from what we have been in a particular career?

Socially and culturally, we can see a similar thing happening with all the discussion at the moment about the date of Australia Day. The question underlying all the discussion is 'who are we?' And are the Aboriginal peoples part of that 'we'? In all important transitions, it is the question of identity that comes to the fore.

Transitions in the Church

When transitions occur in the Church, we can see the same patterns emerging as we see in other human transitions. Transition is always occurring in the life of an historical reality such as the Church. More prominent times of transition are, however, more noticeable in the whole body of the Church and are given greater attention by historians and theologians. I want to mention two of these notable times of transition in particular because of their radical importance – historically and theologically – along with their importance in clarifying Christian identity.

One transition is reflected in the New Testament writings and it is perhaps a paradigm for all other transitions in the Church's history. In those New Testament times, Christianity moved beyond the world of the Bible and of Judaism into the world of the pagan Greco-Roman Empire. Christianity's roots were and are in Judaism. This is obvious from the fact that much of what is important to us today is rooted in the practices of Israel: the word of God in the first covenant, the psalms as our prayer, the structure of the Eucharist, many of our prayer forms and even many of the words that we continue to use.

Yet in the name of Jesus the Christ, Christianity had to move beyond Israel in order to be Christ-ian. We can see ample evidence for this transition in the New Testament: Peter's vision in the house of Cornelius in the Acts of the Apostles (Acts 10:1-33;11:1-18), the gathering of the Christian leaders in Jerusalem to resolve the disputes that had arisen about Gentiles becoming Christians (Acts 15:5-28 and Galatians 2:1-10) and repeatedly throughout the letters of St Paul.

The conflict was between those who thought Christianity should remain within Judaism and those who thought that Christianity had to be open to all the nations. This transition involved a hard fought conflict but the issue had to be resolved if Christianity was to achieve its own proper identity.

Again, beginning in the fourth century, Christianity underwent a radical transition and eventually became the religion of the Roman Empire. This involved a large-scale transition from a Church made up of many small communities which were not recognised by the law and at times under threat. They were intense communities and to enter them required a long and demanding initiation process which we call the Catechumenate. In this transition, Christianity opened its door to all and sundry and within a couple of centuries virtually the whole population of the Roman Empire had become Christian. This christianisation came about not by an intense process of initiation of individuals but by creating a society whose forms and institutions were Christian so that the population would become Christian by social absorption, by a sort of social osmosis.

In this transition, many Christians felt that the Church was losing its identity, that it was being absorbed by the society which, a short time before, had been inimical to it. This transition changed the requirements for baptism, altered the shape of the Eucharist, created a new pastoral strategy and introduced a new social structure in which Christianity and society interpenetrated each other.

There were groups of Christians who separated themselves from the overall Church because of this shift. And it was a contributing factor to the rise of monasticism in which some Christians distanced themselves from the wider society.[1]

Within this transition the language of the Christian faith also underwent changes because the majority of Christians now belonged not to a culture grounded in the Scriptures and Judaism but to the various cultures of the Greco-Roman Empire. So the ways of thought and expression of those cultures entered into the life of the Church. Alongside an expression of the Christian faith which was rooted in the

---

[1] See M. Sheridan, 'Segregati a credentium turba.' Historical and Theological reflections on ecclesial aspects of monastic origins, in *Cristianesimo nella Storia* 36 (2015), 251-275.

Scriptures, we began to see an expression of the same faith cast in the mould of the thought of Greece and Rome.

This way of thinking raised questions that had been dormant before this time. There was a need for a greater clarity about the person of Jesus and about the Trinity, if Christianity was to be genuinely understood within that different culture. In response to the discussions raised about these central mysteries of the faith, the first Ecumenical Councils were called. The major statements of all of them were seeking to clarify the divinity and humanity of Jesus and the meaning of the Trinity as One God of three persons. Each of these ancient Councils – Nicea in 325, Constantinople I in 381, Ephesus in 431 and Chalcedon in 451 – dealt with the same issues that kept rolling on in the midst of further disagreements, divisions and insights.

The above two transitions are of radical importance in the history of all of Christianity. And because they were significant transitions, the question of Christian identity was at stake in each of them. It was at stake in sorting out the identity of Christianity vis-à-vis Judaism. And from the fourth century on, Christian identity required that it sort out its faith in Jesus as the revelation of God. It could not be itself unless that question came to some clarity.

Transition today

The transition in which we are involved today is, by and large, a transition brought about by widespread changes within the societies in which believers live. These changes impact upon the Church not just exteriorly but interiorly because the Church is made up of contemporary people living in these societies and being formed by them.

Christians are always members of the society of which they are part. Consequently any period of Christian history has to be looked at within its own cultural context. This has been so from the beginning of Christianity in the Jewishness of Jesus and his immediate followers.

There is no issue in the Church at the moment that can be considered adequately unless we take into account that we are in a time of quite radical transition.

First and foremost, we are in a transition that is long term. We are moving out of a multi-millennial stretch of time in which it was taken for granted that religion penetrated every aspect of society, that religion was in fact the glue of society and was indispensable to the functioning of any society. This presupposition preceded Christianity; it was true of the religions of antiquity. We have already moved into an epoch in which society and religion have been divorced from each other and religion has come to be seen as a matter for the individual member of society rather than being a matter of the social, cultural and political sphere. This is more obvious in some parts of the Church than others; it affects the Churches of the Western World very sharply. Even in the United States of America, where there is much public talk and acceptance of religion, is not the religion presumed that of individuals?

This divorce between society and religion means that people will no longer be believers simply by being a member of a society which takes the religious dimension of life for granted. In the Christian societies of the past, the basic process by which people became Christian was by means of living in a society which presumed that everyone not only should be but would be Christian. Such a religious society made its members in its own image as do all societies. They work by means of a social osmosis.

Such an osmosis can no longer be in play in a society in which religion and society are divorced from each other. We have moved into societies which are in principle pluralist regarding religion, that is, all religions are recognised and no one religion or worldview is given official recognition over others. So, as said above, the religious option is no longer a social and cultural option but the option of the individual member of the society.

Once this new situation is accepted as the way things are going to be, it means a radical change for the way the Church is and acts. There have to be new forms of evangelisation, that is, new ways of engaging people with faith in Christ. If the question of evangelisation is the most significant issue of our time, there needs to be an evangelising dimension to all that we do including the celebration of the liturgy which is the main subject of this book. The above transition affects every aspect of the life of the Church; it means that so many of our presumptions have to change. Anyone in a pastoral position has had the question put to them countless times: why do our young people not go to Mass? This question cannot be answered without reference to the above transition into a pluralist society.

We can never ignore the fact mentioned above that societies tend to make their members in their own image; this concretises the power of any society over its members. This will affect all the members of the Church and so the faith will have to be passed on and explained much more explicitly and deliberately.

Within this transition we are living, there has also occurred great disillusionment because of the scandal of sexual abuse and its cover up in the Church. It is not only the horrific nature of the abuse and its consequences that has so affected people but the attitudes which lay behind the way the crisis was dealt with: the clericalism, the presumption of power, disdain for the victims and the virtual excusing of offenders.

The reaction to this among so many within the Church as well as outside of it is bringing about a change within the above transition. Many people have lost trust in the leadership of the Church and are seeking a greater part in the way in which decisions are made within the Church. They are no longer content to be a silent and docile majority.

There is another aspect to the transition we are experiencing today and that is the presence and ministry of Pope Francis. He is urging renewal upon the whole Church and doing so strongly and constantly in the documents he writes, the speeches he makes, and the actions he performs. He returns to and develops further the ways of being the Church proposed in the documents of the Second Vatican Council. This reform from above is unsettling those who do not like change and especially those for whom change would spell disadvantage.

The constant reference point for change over the last almost fifty years has been that Second Vatican Council. Despite the fact that there has been ebb and flow in the attitudes of popes, bishops, priests and people to the reforms initiated by that Council, it is a determining event in the life of the Church. It is an Ecumenical Council, that is, the most recognised form of the Catholic Church's expression of its faith. No other documents enjoy the same status as those of an Ecumenical Council.

The Council of Trent was a radically important Ecumenical Council which shaped the centuries that followed it but as studies of its reception show, there were many hesitations about and obstacles to its implementation.[2] A pattern we see repeated in the post-Vatican II period.

As is the case with transitions, this current transition is about the identity of the Catholic Church. There was a renewed discovery of the Christian faith going on at Vatican II and that discovery continues in the Church of this time. As the Council makes clear in its documents, the Church is seeking a new identity with regard to the society in which it lives (see the Document on the Church in the Contemporary World – *Gaudium et Spes*), with regard to other Christian Churches (see the Document on Ecumenism – *Unitatis Reintegratio*), with regard to other religious traditions (see the Document on Non-Christian Religions – *Nostra Aetate*) and in the understanding of its own nature and purpose in the Document on the Church – *Lumen Gentium*).[3]

---

[2] J. W. O'Malley, Trent. *What Happened at the Council?* Cambridge, Massachusetts/London, England: The Belnap Press of Harvard University Press, 3013, esp. pp. 248-275; G. Alberigo, 'From the Council of Trent to 'Tridentinism' in (eds) R. F. Bulman & F. J Parrella, *From Trent to Vatican II*, OUP, 2006, pp. 19-37; M.A. Mullett, *The Catholic Reformation*, London & New York: Routledge,1999.

[3] A Flannery (ed.), *Vatican Council II. The Conciliar and Post Conciliar Documents. New Revised Edition.* Dublin, Ireland/ Newtown NSW, Australia: Dominican Publications/ E. J. Dwyer Pty.Ltd, 1992.

Liturgy

It was in the celebration of the liturgy that the changes proposed by Vatican II were symbolised. The liturgical changes which followed on from the Council were the tip of the iceberg of the changes that were afoot. There was much to come but it was in the liturgy that ordinary Catholics began to come face to face with a new type of Church. As indicated earlier reaction to these changes varied from enthusiastic acceptance through a lukewarm tentativeness to rejection and that sometimes even to the point of schism.

These reactions brought to the surface the inner unexpressed presumptions that people had about what it means to be the Church. It was precisely the celebration of the liturgy which brought these to the surface because in the words and actions of the liturgy a different form of the Church was being proposed and experienced.

To elaborate further on what is being played out in this renewal of the liturgy, I would like to refer again to a saying common in Eucharistic theology: 'The Eucharist makes the Church and the Church makes the Eucharist'. This is a theological statement but it is also a pastoral and practical statement. This saying rightly grounds the identity of the Church in the Eucharist, and expresses the interplay between the Eucharist and the Church. There is implied in this that significant changes in the celebration of the Eucharist will throw up questions about the very nature of the Church.

In accord with this principle, we can see the changes following Vatican II shaping the understanding of who and what the Church is. Vatican II sees the overriding principle of the liturgy's renewal as the full and active participation of the people.[4] This principle and its implementation challenged the earlier practice in which the liturgy was a matter for the clergy. This new principle wrought many changes of attitude in the celebration of the Eucharist and is a seed for further changes in the liturgy and in the overall life of the Church.

A change that aroused some strong reaction was the introduction of the sign of peace at Mass. This put a question to the previous practice that, at Mass, people were to be completely silent and take no notice of the other members of the congregation around them. The sign of peace was suggesting a shift in the understanding of the Mass from one involving an individual participation to one involving communal participation.

The change into vernacular languages opened up the need for communication between the priest and the people. The changed stance of the priest behind the altar likewise embodied a question about the very nature of the Church: are not all of us the Church and does not the Eucharist belong to all of us?

The liturgical changes are about changes in the Church, changes in our understanding of ourselves as the Church. In these changes, the Church is doing the Eucharist and the Eucharist is remaking the Church. Re-forming the liturgy is re-forming the Church.

As in any transition – as we saw above – there is always a human tendency to go back into the security of what we

---

[4] *Sacrosanctum Concilium* (hereafter referred to as S.C.). The Constitution on the Sacred Liturgy, no 14, in Flannery, op. cit., p. 7.

have known and where we feel comfortable but that impedes the necessary transition into the new. In any transition, a decision has to be made to move ahead even if there are fears and dangers involved in that forward movement. In any significant transition we enter into the process of renewing and deepening our sense of identity.

Liturgy in a non-religious society

Liturgy celebrated in a pluralist society will have to take into account the nature of that society. Those participating in the liturgy are shaped by being members of that society. As we have seen above, in such a society religion is seen as an option for the individual members. And the secular thread in any such society may be so strong that it creates an atmosphere in which a religious stance becomes implausible.

Individualism is characteristic of contemporary Western societies: there is a strong emphasis on the importance of the individual's experience and feelings with a de-emphasis on the communal aspects of being human. This can result in religious traditions slipping into individualist forms with little reference to the communal dimension of the tradition. As a consequence, in the Catholic situation 'going to Mass' might not be seen as having much importance over against individual spirituality. Living in a pluralist society will also, therefore, have an influence on the number of people going to Mass, while still identifying as Catholic.

In the centuries of Christendom, being Christian was simply part of being a member of society since that society was socially, culturally and politically Christian. A consequence of this was that there was little need for explicit initiation into the Christian faith as the society into which people were born did that initiating. People became Christian in the same way as people become members of their societies today – by what we have called above a social osmosis. People took it for granted that Christianity was a part of them. As Stephen Bullivant puts it in his book *Mass Exodus*: 'If everyone shares the same beliefs, they are not beliefs, they are just how the world is'.[5] This situation is no longer ours.

In the centuries before the interpenetration of Christianity and society – the first three or four centuries roughly speaking – the catechumenate was an integral part of the life and functioning of the Church. It was the means by which people became Christian and it was a process requiring several years of learning to live and understand the Christian faith.

It was prophetic that following the Second Vatican Council, a catechumenal process was formally introduced into the life of the Church. This was not just for 'mission' countries but for those areas where the Christian faith had been established for centuries. We need such a process in the life of the Church today because the faith will not come 'naturally' to members of our society.

Today, people cannot just walk off the street and know what is happening in the celebration of Mass. They will need some means of entering into the Eucharist and its meaning as did those new Christians of those first centuries. This

---

[5] *Mass Exodus. Catholic Disaffiliation in Britain and America since Vatican II.* OUP, 2019, p. 101.

does not mean that everyone has to become an amateur theologian in order to be Christian but that they need to know what the gift of Jesus Christ means for our being human, which is what the catechumenate does.

The Fathers of the Church had their 'mystagogical' catecheses. This unusual word (mystagogy) referred to the introduction that they gave to their people about the very liturgy or mystery they were all in the course of celebrating.[6] In these our days, we need some means of coming to a sufficiently explicit understanding of our faith to be able to identity as Christian.

Another slippage which easily occurs in our society is that Christianity can be reduced to a matter of morality. In this instance, being Christian comes to mean something like being a good person or 'loving our neighbour' or having 'Christian values'. This reduction can leave aside that critical dimension of the faith found in the mystery of Christ's death and resurrection and indeed in his very person. Christian identity rests in relationship to Jesus Christ, who is the gift of God's self to human beings.

The question of Christian identity is vitally important in pluralist societies. The very fact that we live among people who do not share our faith means that we are driven to ask ourselves more pointedly what it is that we believe, what is this hope that is in us (1 Peter 3:13-16).

---

[6] See G. Boselli, *The Spiritual Meaning of the Liturgy*. Collegeville, Minnesota: Liturgical Press, 2014; E. Mazza, *Mystagogy. A Theology of Liturgy in the Patristic Age*. NY: Pueblo Publishing Company, 1989.

To begin to deepen our understanding of the liturgy and indeed of our own identity as Christians, we move on to look at the liturgy as essentially made up of signs.

Chapter 2

The Liturgy is Celebrated in Signs

> Since, however, the celebration of the Eucharist, like the entire liturgy, is carried out by means of perceptible signs by which faith is nourished, strengthened and expressed, the greatest care is to be taken that those forms and elements proposed by the Church are chosen and arranged, which, given the circumstances of persons and places, more effectively foster active and full participation and more aptly respond to the spiritual needs of the faithful.[7]

THIS QUOTATION FROM THE *Introduction to the Roman Missal* indicates that signs are the medium used in the celebration of the liturgy. The Introduction to the Missal from which this quotation is drawn is an important document which is part of the Missal itself. It gives the outlines

---

[7] *General Instruction of the Roman Missal*, no. 20. Australian Catholic Bishops Conference. Strathfield, NSW: St Pauls, 2012.

of an understanding of the Mass whose rites and texts are given in the rest of the Missal. The above quotation from that document is, in its turn, dependent on the document on the liturgy of the Second Vatican Council.[8]

The point we need to make here is that 'the Eucharist, like the entire liturgy, is carried out by means of perceptible signs...'. What we do in the liturgy is done by means of the signs which have been handed down to us from the beginnings of our tradition or which have been developed in the course of that tradition on the basis of those beginnings.

These signs have a human and biblical background which we need to take into account if we are to use and understand them well. So bread and wine have a background in human cultures that is relevant to their use in the Eucharist. Bread is the food that keeps people alive day by day. Wine, likewise, has roots in human culture as a means of celebrating and as a food which changes our spirit.[9] The biblical tradition in the Old Testament uses those basic human realities in the course of living out its covenant with God. Bread and wine were taken up into the liturgy of the first covenant. Jesus used them in celebrating the liturgy of his people.

Both bread and wine – and for that matter water, oil and the laying on of hands – have deep human and biblical meaning that takes on new significance in the New Testament and in the development of the Christian tradition.

---

[8] S. C. 59.

[9] For a more detailed treatment of this, see F. O'Loughlin, *New Wineskins*. Bayswater, Victoria: Coventry Press, 2019. See also P. Rech OSB. *Wine and Bread*. Chicago: Liturgy Training Publications, 1998, and J. Marquinez, *Wine in the Bible*. San Francisco: Wine Appreciation Guild, 2013.

Sign/symbol – mystery

We have been given signs by means of which to celebrate the Eucharist precisely because we are celebrating a mystery, that is, we are celebrating something that is beyond us.

The word 'mystery' when used in liturgy or theology does not refer to a puzzle or to something to be solved like a murder mystery. Rather, mystery, liturgically and theologically, is something that cannot be worked out; it involves something that is beyond us. We need symbols as our means of communication and communion with that mystery. A mystery, therefore involves a human reality in which we discover something of the Divine. It is something in which the Divine comes across to us not in its own guise but in the guise of the symbol or sign.

This presence of symbol in the liturgy is parallel to the presence of symbols in ancient myths and also in dreams: in these, symbols take human beings beyond themselves to discover something more of themselves. Christian symbols take believers beyond themselves to discover more deeply their relationship with God in Christ.

The mystery of Christ has been confided to us in human realities known to us from our human experience and so their place in our human experience and that of the biblical tradition is crucial to our use and understanding of them.

It is striking that what we have been given are concrete material realities belonging to our world and to our everyday lives. These form the signs with which our communication and communion with Christ is to be accomplished. These signs are the major religious realities handed down in the

Christian tradition. There are, of course, other valuable religious activities such as fasting or pilgrimage or personal meditation, but they are not the primary religious activities which have been given to us from the beginnings of our tradition, and from the Lord himself.

We begin the liturgy of the Eucharist with two blessings, which pray in the following way over the simple gifts of bread and wine:

Blessed are you, Lord God of all creation.
Through your goodness we have this bread (this wine) to offer
which earth has given and human hands have made
(fruit of the vine and work of human hands)
It will become for us the bread of life.
(It will become our spiritual drink).

These human elements of bread and wine are already gifts of God who is creatively at work in the earth's fruitfulness and who continues to work wonderfully through the hands of human beings whom he has created in his image. It is this bread and wine which come from the earth and which human hands have made that will become our ultimate bread of life and the drink that penetrates us and en-Spirits us.

These human things are the essentials of the liturgy. They are the means of communion in the Mystery of God opened up to us in Christ. In the sacraments there is drawn together God at work in his creation and God at work leading that creation beyond itself into the new creation begun in the death and resurrection of Jesus, who is the new human being, the perfect image of the God we cannot see.

Sign and symbol

Over the time between the Reformation and the renewal movements of the twentieth century the understanding of the sacraments and especially of the Eucharist had been caught up in the straightjacket of the bitter controversies between Catholics and Protestants of which we spoke in chapter one. In these controversies, each of the parties became exaggeratedly bonded to their particular position. This brought about inaccurate views of each party's position and tended to block off access to the broader and deeper understandings of the sacraments present in the Scriptures, the Patristic age and in the Middle Ages.

One of the issues caught up in this was that of the understanding of signs. And one of the words set aside by Catholics as unacceptable was that of symbol which in Catholic discourse was normally accompanied by the adjective 'mere' as an indication that such things were considered of no value in understanding the sacraments.

More recent study of symbol by scholars in several different fields of research and most importantly for our purpose by theologians has brought about an appreciation of just how important this concept is for the sacraments and especially for the Eucharist.[10]

---

[10] K. Rahner, 'Theology of the Symbol', *Theological Investigations IV*. London: DLT, 1966, pp. 221-252; L-M Chauvet, *Symbol and Sacrament*, Collegeville,

These studies have brought us to see that the basis of symbol is our own selves. We are bodies and yet we can go beyond our bodies. As persons, we are not locked in our bodies, but we can communicate our selves in a bodily way – that is by means of words and actions. Our words and actions are bodily and yet they communicate our inner personal spiritual self which permeates our body and transcends it. Our actions and words carry us across to one another. They enable us to present ourselves to each other and to know each other.

Words and actions in relation to ourselves are the foundation of what is meant by symbol and the symbolic. We receive each other's *real presence* by means of these words and actions and they are our means of putting ourselves outside of ourselves.

We use words and actions in the liturgy and in the Eucharist these words and actions are said and done over bread and wine which become the means by which we enter into communication and communion with the Lord who has handed these things on to us to do in his memory.

Our own bodiliness by means of which we enter into communion with each other provides the model for understanding our entering into communication and communion with the Lord. The sacraments are to him what our words and actions are to us. This is most fully true of the Eucharist.

Minnesota: Liturgical Press, 1995; and idem, *The Sacraments. The Word of God at the Mercy of the Body*, Collegeville, Minnesota: Liturgical Press, 2001.

Sign, symbol, celebration

In celebrating the liturgy, we need to celebrate it in the precise awareness that we are dealing with symbols. The words and actions of the liturgy seek to go beyond themselves to the mystery being celebrated by their means. By its very nature as sign, the liturgy's words and actions are intended to go beyond themselves. The rites of the liturgy are celebrated as a means of communication and communion with Christ; they are not an end in themselves but a means of entering into the mystery.

Liturgy of the Word

The liturgy of the Word has a symbolic character. It is a celebration, not a lesson. Its signs are the readings we take from the Scriptures. The liturgy of the Word is not just about the texts that are being read but about what those texts arouse in the hearts and minds of those listening. The texts are meant to be provocative in this sense, to raise questions and even doubts, to create puzzlement, to give insight, to console and share the joy of the gospel. The real working of God's word is in the interaction that takes place between the texts and the listeners; this is where the Spirit of God is at work leading us into all truth. The homily is a means of enabling that interaction to take place.

Thus the readings act as signs; they are symbolic texts. They present some encounter between God and human beings from the biblical tradition or some reflection on or consequence of such encounters. The point of recounting such moments from the past is not, first and foremost, about that past but about how that past moment might enable us to discover the same God in the present.

The Liturgy of the Eucharist

In the Eucharist, we take bread and wine out of their usual context in daily life and use them as signs or symbols that speak to us of 'the authentic bread of life' and the 'saving cup' of that new covenant which came about in Christ's dying on the cross and his rising to new life. In the gospel accounts of the Last Supper, bread and wine are taken beyond their Old Testament context to refer to that gift Jesus makes of himself on the cross which gift brings about the new passover.

As said earlier, to enable bread and wine to speak of that which is beyond them, we need to take into account their context in human life. We do not forget that bread is bread and that wine is wine. We do not ignore the context in human life from which they are drawn. We do not ignore their place in the religious life of Israel. We see their new meaning arising out of the interplay between their human meaning, their earlier biblical meaning and their relationship with Jesus Christ.[11]

What bread and wine are in daily life is also associated with God in the Scriptures as it is in our praying of grace at meals. In their simply being what they are, we see them as gifts of God. We recognise this in the blessings of the Preparation of the Gifts at Mass already quoted. In the Eucharist,

---

[11] For a further treatment of this, see Frank O'Loughlin, *New Wineskins*, Bayswater, Victoria: Coventry Press, 2019.

bread and wine become more authentically what they are. They become the means by which life in its fullness begins to come to us.

Symbols within the Eucharist

There is a constitutive symbolic structure to the Eucharist which arises out of the actions of Christ at the Last Supper as recounted in the gospels. So the Eucharistic action is constituted by taking bread and wine at the Presentation of the Gifts, by giving thanks and praise over them in the Eucharistic Prayer, by breaking that bread at the Fraction and by giving that bread and wine at Communion. These symbolic actions constitute the Eucharist; they are essential to it. And each of the elements of bread and wine has embedded in them different approaches to the Mystery being given to us in the Eucharist.[12]

The procession with gifts is the people's way of entering into the action of the Eucharist. It is not just the bread and wine that enters into the mystery of the Eucharist but the people who are symbolised in them and who will receive them back in communion.

In the Eucharistic Prayer, we all give thanks to the Father as Jesus did at the Last Supper. We now give thanks for what the Father has done in the death and resurrection of Jesus in which we will share when we eat this bread and drink this cup over which the prayer is being prayed. And then we pray to the Father that he will bring to completion what

---

[12] Ibid.

The Liturgy is Celebrated in Signs

was begun in that death and resurrection. In the midst of this prayer, we have the account of Jesus' actions and words at the Last Supper which the whole liturgy of the Eucharist embodies in its entire length from the Procession with Gifts to Communion. The entire liturgy of the Eucharist is doing anew the actions of Jesus at that Supper: he takes, blesses, breaks the bread and gives the bread and cup to his disciples.

The breaking of the bread is the one of the actions of the Lord at the Last Supper which we do in his memory and which is constitutive of the whole action. The bread is broken so that it can be what bread is – a source of life. It is broken so that all can share in the one loaf of bread, that is, in the one source of life; and this in order that we may become the one Body of the Christ who was broken on the cross for the life of the world. We pray the Lamb of God during this breaking because the Christ who was broken on the cross is our source of life and unity.

We go to communion as a group to receive this broken bread because this communion is about our unity with Christ and with one another. For this reason, going to communion is done as a procession. We also seek to express that unity by singing as we process to communion. And we receive communion: we don't take communion; we receive it. This is the reason why we stretch out our hands and have the Eucharist placed in them. Similarly we don't take the cup but it is given to us. It is a gift to be received, just as is life itself.

Along with these constitutive and original symbols, there are other highly significant symbols in the Communion Rite. We pray the Lord's Prayer: it is a communion prayer which expresses our union with the Lord and with each other. This finds clear expression in its first word: 'Our'. We don't pray 'my Father' or for that matter 'Father of Jesus'. We pray 'Our Father' because that word expresses our union with the Lord Jesus who gave us the prayer; it also expresses our union with one another.

Then there is the Sign of Peace which is not a mere sign of friendship but a sign of what Christ and his Eucharist seek to bring about among us, to draw us into communion with each other. This communion seeks to go beyond the capacities of human friendship which is dependent on our likes and dislikes. The Greeting of Peace is in the form of a wish. This is so because this peace still struggles to come about among us – it is a peace of which we are not yet capable. To give the sign of peace to those with whom we are in discord brings out its significance as something dependent on the working of God's Spirit among us. It asks us to be open to the possibility of resolving human discord.

All the things we do and say in the Eucharist and the things we use have a symbolic value: they point beyond themselves. The altar or table takes its significance from what is done at it. It and its decoration refer to the Last Supper or to the death of Jesus and his resurrection out of death. The altar is also symbolic of that table in the kingdom of the Father to which we are called and whose coming will be the completion of the Eucharist and its finale. The altar is not a bench or a shelf but is used in accord with its symbolic nature. The construction of the altar is usually in accord with its symbolic nature which is not always the case with its use.

The vestments worn by the priest and some other ministers also fit into this symbolic code. They are worn to express the fact that we are not engaging in practical activity but in symbolic activity. They seek to express the fact that what we are doing is not what it seems to be to sight and hearing and touch but rather that it leads us to things beyond what we can see and touch and hear. All the various things that we use in the liturgy ought similarly be worthy of this symbolic activity pointing and leading us towards the Mystery that is beyond us and yet with us.

Signs/symbols and rubrics

The principle that liturgy is celebrated in signs has a particular importance in our time of transition because we have come out of an era in which the sign nature of the liturgy had fallen into shadow.

There have been times when the signs of the liturgy were interpreted as veils rather than as signs, that is, the signs of the liturgy were seen as hiding the mystery we are celebrating rather than revealing it. The visible dimension of the liturgy was seen as being celebrated at one level but underneath it something else was going on which the externals were hiding. The two dimensions were seen as in parallel rather than as interconnected. The main link between them was that the ritual had to be done correctly and exactly to assure that the mystery was in fact actuated.

After the Council of Trent, the Congregation of Rites was founded in Rome (1588) to carry out the Council's reform of the liturgy. This effected a factual transfer of authority over the liturgy from the bishops to the papacy. There was particular concern at that time about the aberrations which had crept into the liturgy over time.

The principle established by the Congregation of Rites in this regard was that any rites or customs which were less than 200 years old were to be abolished. This left the ancient rites of many European dioceses intact. There was a considerable number of such rites or usages. Some of these persisted down to the early twentieth century. There were twenty-one different local rites in the Church in France in the nineteenth century.

Over the centuries since its foundation, the Congregation of Rites became more and more strict in the regulation of the liturgy. The rubrics became more and more dominant in the celebration of the liturgy.

Rubrics is the name given to the instructions about what to do and what to say in the course of the celebration of the liturgy. The name rubrics comes from the fact that they were printed in red (*ruber* in Latin) in the Missal whereas the texts were printed in black. An increased insistence on the rubrics became a mindset throughout the Western Church which found expression in the detailed and rather scrupulous following of these rubrical instructions. This mentality became so dominant that if the rites were not celebrated with exactitude, the effectiveness of the sacrament was called into question. Practically speaking, this legalist understanding of the Mass set aside its nature as a celebration taking place in the medium of signs.

A different mindset was set forth in the liturgy proposed by the Second Vatican Council and the documents consequent to it. It takes time for a new mentality to work its way into our practice and so the new attitudes proposed have come about in a piecemeal fashion in the practice of the many communities of the Church. In reaction to the tightness of the liturgical practice of the last few centuries, some liturgical practices arose which were not well grounded in the principles of the liturgy. There are also those who are determined not to take seriously the new attitudes proposed by the Council.

Principles and rubrics

The rubrics given in the official books of the liturgy are not irrelevant. They are there to embody basic principles that grow out of the nature of the liturgy. The importance of the rubrics ought to be seen in their relationship to these more basic principles. If the rubrics become more important than the principles, then they have gone beyond their proper domain.

In this area, a problem arises when ministers do not have a grasp of the fundamentals of the liturgy. When this is the case, there can be celebrations of the liturgy which tend to introduce elements into the liturgy which do not gel with its nature. Examples of such elements would be the substitution of non biblical readings for readings from the Scriptures or the use of Eucharistic Prayers which do not have the necessary memorial structure to be a Eucharistic Prayer, or the desire to treat the liturgy as a catechetical lesson rather than a celebration in word and sacrament.

A once common aberration was for the priest to break the bread during the account of the Last Supper (the Consecration) at the words 'he broke it'. This is a misunderstanding of the nature of the Eucharistic liturgy which, as a whole celebration, does what is narrated in the account of the Last Supper. Thus it is at the 'breaking of the bread' or the fraction that the bread should be broken. The liturgy is not drama but symbolic action.

There is no substitute for adequate liturgical formation. This is especially so for ordained ministers, but it is also important for all involved in the liturgy including the celebrating faithful. Just as liturgy can become too ritualistic and formal, so also can it become too conversational and practical. It always remains a symbolic celebration which goes beyond the everyday to shed light on the everyday.

The way in which the liturgy is celebrated especially by ordained ministers needs to be penetrated by the understanding that it is in symbol that it is being celebrated.

Chapter 3

The Work of the People of God

THE LITURGY IS THE CELEBRATION of *the* People of God as a unity, as the body of Christ. The Eucharist in particular is the celebration of the Church gathered into unity. The word for Church in the New Testament (*ekklesia*) is used to describe those whom God has called and gathered to himself from among human beings to play a particular role in God's working among human beings. God's activity in the world is not just for those called into the Church but for all human beings and indeed for the whole of creation. This choosing of a People in view of a wider plan was part of the Mosaic covenant in the Old Testament and it is part of the new and eternal covenant made in and through Jesus the Christ.[13]

Unfortunately, when the word 'Church' is used in common parlance today, it is usually used to indicate the institutional

---

[13] This particular role of the People of God will be dealt with at greater length in Chapter 10 of this book.

Church or the authorities of the Church. We need to be careful not to read this meaning back into the Scriptures, or for that matter into the liturgical texts.

The document on the Church of the Second Vatican Council in its first two chapters deals with 'The Mystery of the Church' and 'The People of God'. It takes up the original understanding of the Church as the whole People of God, which is the body of Christ. Returning to this basic and original meaning of the word 'Church' often requires a deliberate adjustment of our thinking and speaking.

Given that the liturgy is the celebration of the Church as a whole, we need to take account of the way the Church is structured. There are ministers within the assembled people who play crucial roles in its celebrations. Whatever role these ministers play – bishop, priest, deacon, reader, cantor and so on – they exercise that role within the community of the Church and for the community of the Church. They are organs of the Church. There is echoed in this ministerial structure St Paul's image of the Church as a body with many different organs, each having their particular roles.[14]

The past: a clerical liturgy

A look into our past will be useful at this point in order to bring out more clearly by contrast what is meant by speaking of the liturgy as the action of the whole Church and to cast light on some of our current difficulties in reforming both the liturgy and the Church. The contemporary emphasis on

---

[14] See 1 Corinthians 12:4-21.

the liturgy as the work of the whole Church can be difficult to implement because over a great many centuries the liturgy was a matter for the clergy rather than for the whole gathered Church.

There are historical reasons that help to explain why the liturgy became the domain of the clergy. First, when Europe was Christianised in Late Antiquity, large numbers of people became Christian without much in the way of personal initiation. As a rule, the clergy had some education in the faith while for the most part the laity became Christian by being part of an established Christian society, by what we have called above a social osmosis. In effect, this helped to lead to a situation in which lay people were second class Christians.

Secondly, along with this in Western Europe the liturgy was celebrated in Latin. Latin was for a long time the only written language available in Europe. Various European languages gradually emerged from Latin (French, Italian, Spanish...) while others evolved alongside it (the Germanic languages, the Slavic languages). As time went on, the distance between Latin and those languages derived from it or dependent on it became greater until Latin became unrecognisable to the general population.

Thirdly, it also fitted the social ethos of the Middle Ages that the liturgy was a matter for the clergy. At that time, this was not only a practical matter but a mindset. This is evidenced by the fact that the use of Latin was simply not questioned for such a long time. There was no real concern that the liturgy was not celebrated in the language of the people, because it was presumed that they did not have to understand the liturgy: it was a matter for the Latin-speaking clergy.

This was part of the medieval mentality as is explained by the great French medievalist, Georges Duby. He explains that there were three orders in medieval society: the warriors (*bellatores*) who defended and protected society; those who prayed (*oratores*) whose task it was to fulfil the spiritual needs and duties of society (the clergy); and then the workers (*laboratores*) whose task it was to keep the society fed and served. This was an organic conception of medieval society in which the three orders were in interplay with each other.[15] In this mentality it made sense that it was the clergy who were to be concerned with the liturgy and who served the other two orders in doing that. The liturgy was in principle a matter for the clergy.

Our different situation

We live in a very different social and cultural world which is making us look back at our tradition to ask new questions of it. This happens especially at periods of significant cultural transition. In such transitions, we become aware of aspects of our own tradition which have been forgotten or neglected. So it is that, in the wake of the Second Vatican Council, we have rediscovered many elements of our tradition that had fallen into shadow. Paul VI refers to this in his *Introduction to the General Instruction of the Roman Missal*, in which he is

---

[15] G. Duby, *The Three Orders: Feudal Society Imagined*, Chicago: University of Chicago Press, 1980.

talking about the greater knowledge we have today of our past tradition. He says:

> Hence, the 'norm of the holy Fathers' (the criterion for reform) requires not only the preservation of what our immediate forebears have handed on to us, but also an understanding and a more profound pondering of the Church's entire past ages and of all the ways in which her one faith has been expressed in forms of human and social culture so greatly differing among themselves, indeed, as those prevailing in the Semitic, Greek and Latin regions. Moreover this broader view allows us to see how the Holy Spirit endows the People of God with a marvelous fidelity in preserving the unalterable deposit of faith, even though there is a very great variety of prayers and rites.[16]

In the renewed understanding of the liturgy, we have rediscovered in our own tradition the centrality of the Church as a body and so have come to see the role of ministry differently. On the one hand, there was the rediscovery and reinstitution of ancient ministries such as those of deacon, lector, or cantor. On the other hand, this same renewal has shed light on the role of the ordained ministries as ministries exercised not from outside the whole body of the faithful

---

[16] *General Instruction of the Roman Missal.*(Referred to henceforth as GIRM) Final Text. With application for Australia. Strathfield, NSW: St Pauls Publications, no. 9.

but as ministries within the body of the faithful and indeed as organs of that body.[17]

The role of priests and bishops is tied into the very nature of the Church as understood in the Catholic tradition. In that tradition the Church is seen as a communion of communions. The Church is both each particular community and all the communities of the Church in communion with each other throughout the world. Each diocesan Church has a bishop as its head and each bishop belongs to the College of Bishops whose head is the Bishop of Rome, the Pope. Within each diocese there is a body of priests gathered around the bishop who are leaders within that diocese and especially as leaders of those major divisions of the diocese we call parishes.

The point to be made here is that those who preside at the celebration of the Eucharist are those ministers who link the various dimensions of the Church: the priest links parish and diocese and the bishop links the diocese and the universal Church whose head is the Pope.

The Eucharist is the celebration of the Church and the Church's structure is that of a communion of communions so that the bishop and priest preside at the Eucharist because in their respective ways they embody the Church in its local and universal forms. And the importance of this is that the

---

[17] D. N. Power, OMI, *Mission, Ministry, Order. Reading the Tradition in the Present Context*. NY/London: Continuum, 2008 especially pp. 117-235; B-D. Marliangeas, *Clés pour une théologie du ministère*, Paris: Editions Beauchesne, 1978.

Eucharist is the celebration in which the Church expresses its identity and in turn has that identity renewed.[18]

The Eucharist is the celebration of the Church in a twofold way: first, as the celebration of the community gathered together to celebrate it and secondly, as the celebration of the whole Church as a communion of communions. The priest or bishop is not above the Church but a minister within it. And the locally gathered community is not the whole Church by itself but only in its communion with all the other communities of the Church. For this reason, the name of the Pope and of the diocesan Bishop are mentioned in the Eucharistic Prayer along with a reference to all the bishops of the Church.

This structuring fits in with the meaning of the '12' in the New Testament. The account of Pentecost in the Acts of the Apostles (Acts 2:1-13) is revealing on this point. Pentecost is often referred to as the birth of the Church and the presence of the '12' is very significant. The account of Pentecost is immediately preceded by the account of bringing the '11' back to the number twelve again by the election of Matthias to replace Judas. Being twelve is no accident but theologically highly significant.

The '12' takes its significance from the twelve sons of Jacob who were the patriarchs of the twelve tribes of Israel. The tribe and its patriarch tended to merge into one. So in parallel to the Old Testament, we can't just see the twelve as the predecessors of the bishops but also as embodying

---

[18] F. O'Loughlin, 'Priesthood as a Sacrament', *Australasian Catholic Record* 95,2 (2018), pp. 199-209.

the whole People of God of the new covenant. Just as the Old Testament '12' have a double function of leadership and embodiment of the People, so does the '12' of the New Testament.

Pentecost is, therefore, not just the gift of the Spirit to those twelve particular apostles but to the whole People of the new covenant. The Spirit is given to the '12' not to separate them from the rest of the People of God but as representatives and leaders of that People.[19] The same principle applies to the relationship of the bishop and the People of God of the Church led by him and unified in its relation to him.

The liturgical 'we'

Since the liturgy is the action of the gathered Church as a whole, the prayer of the liturgy is prayed in the first person plural, that is, in using the pronouns 'we' and 'us'. And so at the beginning of the Church's great prayer, the Eucharistic Prayer, the priest says, 'Let us give thanks to the Lord our God'. The presiding priest speaks in terms of us as he himself goes on to pray the prayer. This 'us' is built into the whole Eucharistic Prayer, as it is in all the prayers of the liturgy. The prayer of the liturgy is the prayer of the whole community; the presiding priest gives voice to that prayer. The liturgy is always what the very word itself means etymologically: the work of the People.

---

[19] See J. Schlosser, *Le groupe des Douze. Les lueurs de l'histoire*. Paris: Cerf, 2014.

It is the whole gathered Church at Eucharist that is doing what Jesus commanded it to do in his memory. The whole Church is obeying his word, as the Third Eucharistic Prayer puts it: '... at whose command we celebrate these mysteries' as the earlier English translation of the Roman Missal puts it. Within the celebration of the Eucharist, the priest has the unique role of saying the words and doing the actions that Jesus said and did at the Last Supper. The priest acts as the sign of Christ in whose memory we pray this prayer and in communion with whom we pray this prayer.

The celebration of the Eucharist is the means by which the whole Church enters into continuing communication and communion with its Lord so that it may be what it is – the body of Christ as St Paul would put it. We go back to the Eucharist time and again so that we may be penetrated and possessed by the One who is raising up a body for himself as we celebrate the Eucharist. The priest is there to serve this communion between Christ and his people.

In describing his role with regard to the Lord in John 3:29, John the Baptist gives us a good image we can use to understand the role of the bishop or priest in particular: 'The bride is only for the bridegroom; and yet the bridegroom's friend, who stands there and listens, is glad when he hears the bridegroom's voice'. The covenant between Christ and his Church (his People) is described in the image of bridegroom and bride (Ephesians 5:21-33) as was the relationship between God and his People in the Old Testament. And is not the bridegroom's friend a fine image for the role of bishop and priest, knowing when to step forward and when to step back.

Chapter 4

The Sunday Eucharist

WITH THE EMERGENCE OF CHRISTIANITY as clearly separate from Judaism in the decades following the death and resurrection of Jesus, there was a concomitant shift from celebrating the Jewish Sabbath on the last day of the week to the Christian celebration of the resurrection of Jesus on the first day of the week, that is Sunday. This shift occurred differently in Judeo-Christian circles to Gentile-Christian circles. The more distinctive Christianity became, the more did Sunday become the day of Christians.

This shift occurred, of course, due to the disciples' discovery of the risen Jesus after his death on that first day of the week. Sunday became the day on which Christians gathered together. Their faith was centred on the risen Jesus; they believed – to use St Paul's words – that if Christ was not risen, their faith was in vain (1 Corinthians 15:16-17).

There is a story related about the Abitanian martyrs who died in Turin in about 304. In this story, these martyrs refer to their Sunday gathering as the 'Dominicum', a Latin word which just means 'The Lord's', without any further specification regarding the Lord's 'what'. It is this gathering that the martyrs refuse to give up in the face of persecution because without it they cannot be who they are – Christians. The 'Dominicum' – as we could also call our Sunday gatherings – has three dimensions to it, all of which emphasise its focus upon Christ. These three dimensions are that we gather on the *Lord's day* as the *Lord's people* to celebrate the *Lord's supper*. It is the day which is indeed 'the Lord's'. These three dimensions are all necessary if we are to understand the centrality of the Sunday Eucharist.

It was at this celebration that the Lord continued to give life to his disciples, to make them 'his own'(see John 13:1). At the Lord's Supper, they became the body which Jesus was now raising up for himself.

Sunday is the original Christian feast day. It was and is crucial. It is the means by which the group of disciples become just that, the group centred on the person of Jesus, a group that came to be called the Church which in its Greek original *ekklesia* – as we saw above – means those called together to belong to the Lord in a new way. They are 'the Lord's'.

To draw out the meaning of this, the Fathers of the Church used the phrase referred to earlier: The Eucharist makes the Church and the Church makes the Eucharist. The Eucharist makes the Church what it essentially is – a communion of life with and in Jesus Christ. At the Eucharist, the gathered disciples of Jesus Christ again and again enter into communion with him to become more and more what they are, a communion of life with Christ which St Paul calls the 'body' of Christ. This comes about through our continual listening to his word and our entry into communion with him through the bread and wine of the Eucharist. He enters into us spiritually as bread and wine enter into us physically. He becomes one with us as the bread and wine become one with our bodies.

It was only much later that Sunday Mass became a legal obligation for Christians.[20] What lay behind that law was an insistence on the importance that Sunday Eucharist had for Christians. To absent yourself from it was to remove yourself from the 'body' of Christ, to cut yourself off from the source of continuing to become Christian.[21] This link between Eucharist and Church is what sets the Sunday Eucharist above any other form of the celebration of Mass. It makes it qualitatively different from Mass celebrated on weekdays or on any other occasion. The Sunday Mass has built into it a call to all who are part of the Church to gather together. Other Masses do not have this same call built into them. So it is that Sunday Mass has additional theological meaning to any other celebration of the Eucharist. Weekday Masses – or Masses on other occasions – are by their nature optional. They are devotional rather than strictly ecclesial.

In a pluralist culture

Sunday Mass becomes even more important now that we live in a pluralist culture which does not offer social/cultural

---

[20] See *New Catholic Encyclopaedia. Second Edition*, Washington DC: Catholic University of America 2003. NY: McGraw Hill Book Co. Vol. 13, pp. 609ff. Also of interest: D. Perron, *Histoire du repos dominical*. Paris: L'Harmattan, 2010.

[21] See F. Cassingena-Trevedy, *Les Pères de L'Eglise et la liturgie*. Paris: Artege, 2016, p 41-58.

backup to any particular religious tradition as did societies in the past. Being a Christian today is an option for people.[22]

All societies, all cultures tend to make their members in their own image. Medieval culture made its members in its own Catholic image. Contemporary cultures will tend to ingrain pluralist attitudes in their members. They presume that people are free to adopt or not any way of understanding and living life that is available within it.

Because of this, Christians today are in a position not unlike that of the Christians of the first three centuries. We do live and will continue to live in a society whose culture will not propose Christianity to its members. This raises the question of how believers are to be nourished in their faith in such a cultural setting.

To this question one of the primary answers is attendance at the gathering of the Christian community for the Eucharist. Just as those first Christians needed that Sunday gathering to keep their faith in Christ nourished, so the Sunday Eucharist will become more and more crucial to the maintaining, nourishing and developing of the Christian faith and its communities as we move into the future. The external social and cultural structures are no longer present to act as a scaffolding for the up-building of faith, so there needs to be interior means of building up faith in Christ. This carries the implication that we have to take our celebrations of the Sunday Eucharist seriously and to enable them to develop the faith of the People of God.

---

[22] H. Joas, *Faith as an Option. Possible Futures for Christianity*. Stanford, California: Stanford University Press, 2016.

It is at the Sunday Eucharist that the four things to which the first Christians were called to be faithful in the Acts of the Apostles (Acts 2:42) are available for contemporary Christians. In the above passage from the Acts of the Apostles, the author suggests that those first Christians needed to be 'faithful to the teaching of the Apostles, to the fellowship, to the breaking of the bread and to the prayers'.

For us now, these four things are the gospels (the teaching of the apostles), the community of the Church (the fellowship), the Eucharist (the breaking of the bread) and prayer (the prayers). In the Sunday Mass, all four of these things are drawn together as the Church gathers. Each of these are present in the life of the Church outside the Sunday Mass and Christ will make his influence felt by their means but it is at the Sunday gathering that all four are drawn together to re-enforce each other.

We have to have constant recourse to the gospels, along with the rest of the Scriptures which give the gospels their context. Therein we keep listening for the word of God echoing down to us in all our new historical situations.

We need the community of faith, the Church which is 'us'. This is the context of our faith and where we find our faith reflected back to us in others. The Christian faith involves a personal journey but not a purely individual journey; it is journey on which we are drawn together. This is emphasised in the new vision of the Church expressed in the first paragraph of Vatican II's document on the Church: 'By her relationship with Christ, the Church is a kind of sacrament or sign of intimate union with God and the unity of all mankind (*sic*): she is also the instrument of such union and unity'.

And, if we think about it, our faith comes to us in one way or another from that community we call the Church.

We need the Eucharist. It is what has been bequeathed to us in a uniquely explicit way. The New Testament's 'Do this in memory of me' is a word from the Lord which the Church has taken seriously from the beginning to our own present time. It is the richest and most intense form of the Lord's presence among us.

Finally we need prayer. Without prayer – in its many and varied forms – the Christian faith does not take root in us. It does not get interiorised. Prayer is lifting up our hearts to God that he may enter into us and make us his own. It enables the gospels, the community of the Church and the Eucharist to be interiorly significant to us.

I am sure that there are many Catholics who will struggle with what I am saying in this chapter because they struggle with unsatisfactory celebrations of the Eucharist. Celebrations in which they find little nourishment; or celebrations which ignore the world in which they live out their faith, or celebrations which are in an English which is arcane or complicated or hard to understand, or again celebrations in which there is little feel for the symbolic or the spiritual.

This can indeed be highly frustrating and there is often no immediate resolution of that problem at hand. Such a situation ought to raise questions about how our priests and other ministers are formed and indeed what opportunity is given to all the faithful to understand what the Mass means.

This centrality of the Sunday Eucharist provides a criterion for discerning the very meaning of being Christian, which always comes back to the centrality of the person, death and resurrection of Jesus Christ. The core of our faith is our communion with that Christ which is concentrated in the Sunday Eucharist. In the early centuries when people could not get to the Sunday Mass, communion was taken to them from that Mass. The Sunday Mass was extended to them. And we seek to do this again today. Being a Christian is not *specifically* being a good person but being a believer in Christ and in his death and resurrection.

Looking back to the gospels, we see that they are all centred on the person and work of Jesus. From the beginning to the end of each of them, it is person of Jesus who is the centre of attention. They would never have been written but for his resurrection which shines back into the whole of each of the gospels even though it is recounted at the end. It is himself and his death and resurrection with which all the gospels and indeed all the other New Testament documents are concerned. This is not something we can pass over or put aside. He is the essence of our faith and without him our faith *is* indeed in vain.

Every celebration of the Mass calls us to listen and respond to him as those people presented in the gospels narratives listened and responded to him. Just as every celebration of the Mass calls us to sit at table with him as did those in the gospel times and so enter into communion with him.

Alternatives to Sunday Eucharist

Given the current circumstances in which the Church finds itself, we need to take into account the predicament facing so many Catholics who are unable to have Mass on Sundays.

One option for such communities is to have another celebration in place of the Eucharist which is usually a Celebration of the Word followed by communion in already consecrated Eucharistic bread.

The criterion to be kept in mind for deciding on having such celebrations is still that of the 'Dominicum'. When it is not possible to have the Dominicum with its three dimensions – the gathering of the Lord's people on the Lord's day to celebrate the Lord's Supper – then one ought seek to achieve as much of the Dominicum as is possible. If we cannot have the Lord's Supper, then we seek to have another celebration that gathers the Lord's people together on the Lord's day and we seek another means to articulate the Lord's presence – the celebration of his word.

When this is followed by communion by means of the already consecrated Eucharist, we ought to make explicit the link between the Eucharist we are to receive and the Eucharistic celebration at which the Eucharistic breads were consecrated.

Another possible solution when Catholics find themselves unable to have the Eucharist is to opt to have the Lord's Supper on a day other than Sunday. As I hope I have made clear in what has been said above, there is an importance to Sunday which cannot be passed over; but equally we need to attend to the practical difficulties we face.

I would make the following suggestion in this regard and I do so to maintain the core importance of Sunday.

When Christians first began to celebrate the resurrection at passover time, there was only one celebration that involved a vigil and a time of fasting leading up to the celebration of the Eucharist at dawn on Easter Sunday morning. With the passing of time, this became the Easter Triduum, the three day celebration stretching from the Mass of the Lord's Supper on Holy Thursday night through Good Friday, Holy Saturday and the Mass of the Vigil to Evening Prayer on Easter Sunday.

I would suggest that we could find a model in this expansion of the Easter celebration of the resurrection for an expansion of the Sunday celebration of the resurrection. Could we not spread the celebration of Sunday Eucharists from the Thursday night through to the Sunday? It offers a way of grounding the celebration of the Eucharist in the original feast of the Church – Sunday.

I would make this suggestion only for those difficult situations where it is not possible to celebrate Mass on a Sunday.

Chapter 5

Liturgical Prayer

IN CHAPTER THREE OF THIS BOOK, we looked at the liturgy as the celebration of the Church as the gathered People of God, as a unity. We saw that the liturgy is celebrated in the first person plural, that is, using the pronouns 'we' and 'us'. The use of these pronouns is in tune with the meaning of the word 'liturgy' which comes from two Greek words meaning 'people' and 'work'. It is in its very nature 'the work of the people'. This needs to be manifested in the actual words and actions of the liturgy.

The Church is not just an anonymous crowd of individuals but an organic unity like the parts of the body as St Paul images that unity. As we have seen above, there are – within the Church – acknowledged and ordained leaders whose ministry is integral to the living and working of the People of God. Bishops and priests are ministers of the unity of the Church and as such are signs of Christ. The bishop or priest praying the prayers of the liturgy is in fact a sign of the Church's unity around Christ, a sign that this community is the gathered Church of Christ.

These ministries have considerable pastoral impact. They are symbolic ministries and as such the way they are played out can help or hinder the various members' identification with the Church.

A journey of conversion

That the liturgy is a communal prayer is very important because none of us is yet Christian. We are all – people, priest, bishop – on a journey of conversion. We are in union with Christ and also we are not yet in union with Christ: we are on our pilgrim way. And so we both pray and we are learning to pray.

It is of the nature of the Church that we are pilgrims on a journey to a future promised us. This involves us in a process of conversion which does not end until we are at home with God. Being on this journey, the Church is incomplete and will always be in need of conversion and renewal. We are, as St Paul might say, seeking to move into the mind of Christ (Philippians 2:1-11).

This movement needs to be reflected in the prayer of the Church. Our liturgical prayer is a bridge between where we are now and where we are called to be. The actual prayers of the liturgy are seeking to be a bridge between us as we are now and us as we move into the mind of Christ. So our prayer ought to be taking us a step forward in our journey of conversion. And the moments of silence in the liturgy are crucial moments for us as individuals to enter into this process.

Conversion is a crucial word. The Greek word used for it in the New Testament is *metanoia* whose roots are in two Greek words meaning 'beyond' and 'mind or mindset'. So in our prayer – as in our life – we seek to go beyond our present thoughts and attitudes.

As we know, prayer does not necessarily produce an immediate answer to our need. It is more likely to take us beyond our need into attitudes of 'your will be done' (Matthew 6:10; 24:38) and 'Into your hands I commend my spirit' (Luke 23:46). Our prayer may begin in our needfulness but its direction will take us beyond that into trust in the care of God. As the classic gospel passage has it: 'Ask, and it will be given you; search, and you will find; knock, and the door will be opened for you. For everyone who asks receives, and everyone who searches finds; and for everyone who knocks, the door will be opened', (Luke 11.9-10). This passage speaks of asking and searching but it does not specify what will be given or what will be found. Prayer takes us out of our own ways and leads us into the ways of God. This is true of our personal prayer, as it is of our communal, liturgical prayer. All our prayer is grounded in and leads towards conversion.

Liturgical prayer

Our liturgical prayer grows out of the Scriptures[23] and it has developed as part of our living tradition which has a history

---

[23] Edward Sri, *A Biblical Walk through the Mass*. West Chester: Pennsylvania: Ascension Press, 2010; L-M. Chauvet, *Symbol and Sacrament*. Collegeville, Minnesota: Liturgical Press,1995, pp. 190-227.

of continuity in change. Noticeably the liturgical prayers do not usually repeat the Scriptures but refer to them and have their roots in them. We can see this principle of continuity in change at work in the *Missal of Paul VI* and he refers to it in his *Introduction to the Missal* as we have seen above.[24]

Our liturgical prayers also need to be culturally attuned. In order to lead us in our journey of faith, they have to be able to have impact on the community that prays them.

Many of our liturgical prayers have their origins in a distant time and culture and they show the marks of those origins. The First Eucharistic Prayer (The Roman Canon) is a prime example of this. It is quite unusual among ancient Eucharistic Prayers; its origins are rather obscure but it does show some indications of having Jewish origins, which is not surprising as the origins of the early Church in Rome seem to have been strongly Jewish. The prayer's language and imagery is set within that culture which in fact makes it obscure for Catholics of today.

There are also difficulties with more recent prayer forms such as those produced after the Second Vatican Council because much of their vocabulary and imagery is foreign to the culture of contemporary people. The production of such texts is not an easy task but one upon which we need to be engaged, using the expertise available to us throughout the Church. It needs to involve a process of learning as we go and a readiness to revise work already done.

The lack of immediacy in our liturgical prayer was not a problem over those many centuries when the liturgy was

---

[24] GIRM nos 6-9.

a matter for the clergy alone. But now greater immediacy is necessary since the aim to be considered above all else in liturgical renewal is the full and active participation of the people.[25] This participation is not just in words said and actions done but in mind and heart. The liturgical prayers cannot act as a bridge for the pilgrimage of conversion if they cannot find a starting point in the minds of the Christian people today.

'The true Christian spirit'

The heading of this section is taken from Vatican II's document on the liturgy which reads: 'In the restoration and promotion of the Sacred liturgy, the full and active participation by all the people is the aim to be considered above all else; for it is the primary and indispensable source from which the faithful are to draw the true Christian spirit.'[26]

This is a powerful and arresting statement and in some ways a disturbing one. If the liturgy is not a real part of the lives of the People of God, is their spirit sufficiently Christian?

Over many centuries, the people attending Mass were taken up with their own particular devotions. In that liturgical arrangement, there was and there was supposed to be a parallel praying between the ministers and the people; they prayed along two different lines which went on in parallel but did not cross each other except at moments like

---

[25] S.C. 14, para. 2
[26] S.C. 14, para 2.

the Consecration when bells were rung to draw the people's attention to the liturgical action. In this type of ritual, a certain disengagement between the priest and the people was intentional. The liturgy as proposed by Vatican II calls for the people to be involved directly in the liturgy itself. It calls for the people to be involved in its actions and in its words in accord with their baptismal dignity. They are the priestly People of God. In the New Testament it is the people as a whole who are called priestly not the ministers of the Church. It is the role of ministers – ordained and non-ordained – to serve the priesthood of the People of God. The ministry that came to be called *priesthood* is indeed *ministerial*. Such ministers are called to be a sign of Christ within that priestly People, which is the body that Christ has raised up for himself.

What is the true Christian spirit? To answer this question, we need to look at what the liturgy of the Church offers to us and most especially what the celebration of the Eucharist offers us. Therein we will find the true Christian spirit. It is the celebration of the Eucharist that the Church becomes what it is; and it is in that same celebration that the Church expresses its true identity. It is therein that we discover the true Christian spirit.

In the light of the Eucharist we can say that the true Christian spirit has roots in our constant entry into dialogue with the Scriptures. This spirit grows out of that scriptural encounter with Christ who brings to a climax the gradual unveiling of God throughout the history of the People of God of both testaments. This contact with the Scriptures is always a dialogue because we enter into it as contemporary people who bring new attitudes and questions to the biblical texts.

In that same Eucharistic light, we can see that the Christian spirit has to do with entering into communion with Christ and with each other so forcefully expressed in the liturgy of the Eucharist. This is a communal act in which the whole gathered people is acting as 'the body of Christ'.

The true Christian spirit is also paschal, that is, it is grounded in the passover of Jesus through death into resurrection. In the Eucharist, we share in his passover from human life through death into human life beyond that life as we know it. There is more to be said about the true Christian spirit but these three are the pillars of that spirit.

This implies a movement away from the ways in which people used to be present at Mass. In place of direct participation in the liturgy proposed today, people used to pray their own particular prayers. Such prayers may have been saying the Rosary or one of many other forms of devotion available throughout the centuries. More recently, during the earlier twentieth century, people used small missals translated into the various vernacular languages by which they followed what the priest was praying in the liturgy in Latin. Even though the use of such missals was a step forward, their very use shows how far the practice of the Church had wandered from its 'true Christian spirit'.

A pathway

If the prayers of the liturgy are to be a pathway leading into the true Christian spirit, they need to be comprehensible to the people in such a way that they can identify what the prayer actually prays.

The vocabulary and even more importantly the imagery reflected in the present prayers is already problematic, and it is a problem which will take time and effort to sort out. We need the necessary historical scholarship to understand the texts in their original version and in the forms they have taken in the course of history. And we need the expertise of historians, liturgists and people skilled in the various languages involved. Producing prayerful, imaginative and usable texts requires time and some experimentation but it is a necessary task for the Church's future.

The more recent English translation of the Roman Missal (2010) is a clear step backwards in the production of adequate texts. It lacks clarity, beauty and an appreciation of the English language. It is an act of disrespect for the involvement of the faithful in the liturgy. One has to wonder what its producers had in mind! There is a very considerable problem with the capacity of this translation to connect with the actual imagination which inhabits contemporary minds.[27] The quality of the texts matters because the liturgy is about the direct participation of the People of God!

Liturgical prayer and posture

Various postures are indicated in the Order of Mass for both the ministers and the people to accompany the various attitudes embodied in that part of the Mass. Common bodily

---

[27] For interesting insights into social imagination, see Charles Taylor, *Modern Social Imaginaries*. Durham / London: Duke University Press, 2004.

posture is seen as a sign of the unity of the gathered Church, a sign that this is communal prayer rather than individual prayer.[28]

All liturgical prayer is accompanied by a posture. There is a definite significance embodied in each posture and that significance is derived from the use of the same posture in our lives outside the liturgy. There is a specific reason behind the use of each position in the celebration of the liturgy. We sit to listen to the word of God – we are taking in the word; we stand to pray – we stand up to explicitly address God; we bow – we give honour to significant people and things; we formally walk (process) to communion – we go to meet the Lord and we do this in unity.

There is one posture or stance that I want to emphasise in particular because it is integral to the trust of this whole book. And that is the stance of the people during the Eucharistic Prayer.

In those parts of the liturgy when the People of God is explicitly praying, the whole community stands. The exception to this is during the Eucharistic Prayer.

During the celebration of the liturgy of the Eucharist, the original posture of the people was that of standing. That is still the basic posture indicated for the Eucharistic Prayer in the *General Instruction of the Missal* with the exception of kneeling during the Consecration.[29] Standing was particularly insisted upon on Sundays and during the Easter Season as both are feasts of the resurrection of the Lord.

---

[28] GIRM no. 42.
[29] GIRM no. 43.

Standing, like all the liturgy, is symbolic. Standing is the posture for being ready for *action*. During the Eucharistic Prayer, we are invited to enter into the mystery of Christ's death and resurrection, to place ourselves before the Father in trust and abandonment, to hang with Christ upon the cross as St Paul might put it. It is a time for contemplative action in union with Christ rather than a time of adoration or of withdrawal into individual meditation. The Eucharistic Prayer is the People's prayer. They license the priest to go ahead with it in their 'It is right and fitting to do so' and they put their signature to it in the Great Amen at its end.

The Assembly's 'Amen' at the end of the Eucharistic Prayer parallels their 'Amen' at receiving Communion. This is their agreement to all that has been said and done in the Eucharist. That 'Amen' is the Assembly's agreement to entering into communion with Christ. It is their agreement to being involved with God in his project of bringing the world to himself. They have become one 'through, with and in' Christ before the Father and are renewed as the body of Christ.

Patristic Study has shown the symbolic value and importance that the Fathers of the Church saw in the stance of the Christian community at Eucharist.[30] The Fathers of the Church saw the gesture of standing as indicative of three things. First, of the dignity of human beings as being able to stand before God and look to the heavens as only human

---

[30] F. Cassingena –Travedy, *Le sens du geste liturgique chez les pères de l'église*, MD 293 (2018, 3), 57-74; P. Pretot, *Le liturgie, une experience corporelle*, MD 247 (2006, 3), 7-36.

beings can do. Secondly, they saw this gesture as having particularly Christian significance in contrast to the surrounding pagan religions: Christians do not grovel before God but stand before his face and look God in the eye, so to speak. Thirdly, it represents the resurrection of Jesus. It is with the risen Jesus who has stood up out of the grave that we come before the Father. This is particularly significant on Sundays, the original feast of the resurrection, on Easter Sunday and in the Easter Season all of which celebrate the resurrection of the Lord Jesus.

This is not a trivial question. It is about the dignity of the People of God. They are indeed 'a chosen race, a royal priesthood, a consecrated nation, a people set apart to sing the praises of God who has called them out of darkness into his own most wonderful light' (1 Peter 2:9).

Is not the matter of the stance of the people gathered together something we need to look at in continuing the reform of the liturgy? The medieval overemphasis on the moment of consecration still lingers among us at least in the realm of posture. This tends to see the earlier part of the Eucharistic Prayer as a lead up to the important moment of the consecration and the later part as a corollary of it, which misinterprets the reality of the Eucharist.

The role of the priest-celebrant

The liturgy needs to be celebrated as an act of the whole People of God. Within this celebration the priest has an essential role. He ministers within this action of the whole gathered community of faith. How priests fulfil this role is crucial. As said above, as a symbolic person he has much to do with the way the members of the community of faith can find and strengthen their identification with the Church.

So the liturgy is not the priest's prayer in which the people participate but the whole people's prayer in which the priest has a role of distinctive leadership. This may require a change of mentality for some priests who have inherited a mindset that sees the Mass as basically the business of the priest. They may even have been taught to think that way in their formation. It also requires a change of mindset for many lay people who may not have had the opportunity to deepen their appreciation of the Mass.

Chapter 6
Already but not yet

OFTEN THERE CAN SEEM TO BE A CONFLICT between the words and actions of the liturgy and our experience of life. Quite apart from the difficulties of language and imagery, the prayers of the liturgy can be saying things that do not in fact appear to be true. For instance the *First Preface for Ordinary Sundays of the Year* reads: 'Through his cross and resurrection he (Jesus Christ) freed us from sin and death and called us to the glory that has made us a chosen race, a royal priesthood, a holy nation, a people set apart'. These are lovely words, but are they true? Are we free from sin and death? Do we not experience sin and death as really existing, disturbing realities in our lives? What can a prayer making such claims actually mean? I use the above prayer simply as an example. It illustrates something that is a constant element in the liturgy.

What is being expressed in such prayers brings to the fore a dimension built into the Christian faith of which we are, by and large, insufficiently aware. There is a dimension to Christianity of its very nature which is described by the title of this chapter: 'Already but not yet'. In theological terms, this is called the 'eschatological tension', meaning that we believe that the redemption and healing of humankind has already happened; it has happened in the human being Jesus Christ who is risen and in glory. And what has happened in him God offers to and seeks to bring about for all humankind. But very obviously this has not yet happened either in the Church or among human beings generally. We are on a journey into that future; but it is a future that God has already brought about – but in the person of Jesus Christ.

The Church, the People of God, lives in the present and yet is caught up in a tension toward that future which God is seeking to give to us and to all. The Spirit who creates this tension is at work and is seeking to penetrate both the People of God and humankind. What is specific to the People of Christ is that this tension between human beings as they are now and the future to which they are called is made explicit. Despite its evident failures, both institutional and personal, the Church is not called to live for its own self, but for 'the many', for all human beings upon whom God seeks to bestow his future.[31]

The Church is human and has within it all that humankind has within it, of good and of ill. What is different or new in the Church is this tension, this pull, created by the explicit call of Jesus Christ and by the power of his Spirit. That call and that Spirit will not cease to be effective among those human beings who make up the Church. This is the gravitational pull of Jesus Christ upon human beings which finds its expression in those human beings who have come to know

---

[31] This will be dealt with more explicitly in chapter 10 of this book.

him. It is the reciprocal character of their relationship to Christ that makes this group of human beings different.

From this perspective, on the one hand we are already redeemed; but on the other, we are not yet redeemed. Similarly, death is already overcome but is not as yet overcome. Evil is already overcome but it is not yet overcome. We are already holy but clearly we are not yet holy. We are already called to glory but we are not yet in glory.

This tension grows out of the reality that Jesus was not accepted by human beings but was found wanting and was rejected. The kingdom of God that he preached and acted out did not come about in his time. This human rejection however did not meet with divine rejection but with a change of strategy and a new initiative on God's part.

This new initiative consisted in the resurrection of Jesus as the coming of God's kingdom in his person and in the new outpouring of his Holy Spirit upon humankind. That Spirit would be God's 'presence and action in the world'. This is a new giving of the Spirit who seeks to bring about now what Jesus sought to bring about in his coming among us. John's Gospel tells us that all that the Spirit gives us will be taken from what is Christ's (John 16:13-15). The Spirit is God's presence and action in the *world*.

The Spirit is at work in the whole of creation. The prophetic Spirit given specifically to believers is the gift of being able to recognise the working of the Spirit in all human beings. The signs of this working of the Spirit in the world find expression in the Beatitudes, each of which indicates where God's blessing is at work: in the poor in spirit, the gentle, those who thirst for justice, etc.

This working of the Spirit is expressed beautifully in the *Preface of the Second Eucharistic Prayer of Reconciliation*:

In the midst of conflict and division,
we know it is you
who turn our minds to thoughts of peace.
Your Spirit changes our hearts:
enemies begin to speak to one another,
those estranged join hands in friendship,
and nations seek the way of peace together.
Your Spirit is at work
when understanding puts an end to strife,
when hatred is quenched by mercy,
and vengeance gives way to forgiveness.

Our liturgical prayer is always caught up in this dynamic of 'already but not yet'. In our prayer we constantly make the claim that Christ is victorious over evil and death and we keep celebrating that victory, but we do this in the midst of all that is part of our present concrete lives. We do it, presenting that death and resurrection as the future intended by God for all human beings. And we present that death and resurrection as the source of the Spirit who is God's presence and action in the world. There is always a tension in Christian prayer and Christian life between who and what we are now and who and what we are called to be. And sometimes the difference between the two is scandalous.

All our prayers conclude 'through Christ our Lord', or an equivalent formula. It is through, with and in Christ that we pray and that we act in the world. The Eucharistic Prayer, the most central prayer of the whole of the liturgy, is of course a prayer of thanksgiving for what God has done in Christ but it also calls upon the Spirit to come in the present and the prayer concludes in the Intercessions which pray that God will complete what he has begun in Christ's death and resurrection. This is ingrained in the nature of the Eucharist and the Church as embodying the tension of 'already but not yet'.

Similarly, the Eucharist is tensed between Christ's death and his future coming. 'Whenever you eat this bread, then, and drink this cup, you are proclaiming the Lord's death until he comes' (1 Corinthians 11:26). The Eucharist is stretched between these two moments. They are its two essential reference points: its origin and its end. We receive the gifts that issue from his death – whose other face is his resurrection – but they are not fully received yet. One of the ways used by the Fathers of the Church to describe the Eucharist was that it is God's deposit on the things to come. This offers us a fruitful way of speaking of Christ's relation to the Church in the Eucharist and that is in terms of the anticipation of his Coming. He comes to us in word, in ministry, in the community of believers and in the breaking of the bread, the Eucharist.

The Eucharist is an anticipation of what is to come. It is the deposit God puts down as the beginning of what he has in store for us, so often imaged as a banquet. That future 'banquet' is the fulfillment of the Eucharist.

We often describe the Church as 'holy' as does the Creed: 'I believe in the Holy Spirit, the holy catholic Church...'. Do we not get something of a jolt when we hear these words? Often we are impressed not by the holiness of the Church but by its (our) sinfulness. This is again a dimension of the 'already but not yet' dynamic. Holiness is already present among us because we the Church are in communion with God in Christ as an essential part of our reality. Holiness biblically is not so much a subjective quality of particular persons but a quality associated with the presence of God whose particular quality it is. We proclaim God to be 'Holy, Holy, Holy'.

The community of the Church is also sinful. This sinfulness became evident in the earliest Church which gradually set up structures to deal with the serious instances of sinfulness as they occurred in the life of the Church. Forms of penance arose as part of the ritual structures of the Church. Presumably some people left the Church because of their infidelity and there would have been others who would have insisted that they should. On the other hand, there were those who had seriously sinned but who remained convinced Christians and desired to remain part of the Church. For these there came about gradually and in piecemeal fashion the first form of penance in the history of the Church. This took the form of temporary exclusion from the community followed by a virtual repetition of the process of the catechumenate by which they had first became Christians. This was the initial form of penance which then developed in many forms over the course of the centuries.[32] These structures

---

[32] See J. Dallen, *The Reconciling Community. The Rite of Penance*. NY: Pueblo Publishing Company, 1974; Favazza J. A., *The Order of Penitents. Historical Roots and Pastoral Future*. Collegeville, Minnesota: Liturgical Press, 1988; F. O'Loughlin, *The Future of the Sacrament of Penance*, Strathfield, NSW: St Pauls, 2007.

each in their own particular way express and make concrete the tension in the Church between holiness and sinfulness.

There is a parallel pattern at work in the sacrament of the Anointing of the Sick. We see this sacrament in continuity with the miracles of Jesus recounted in the gospels: in his miracles the kingdom of God came among human beings. These miracles gave form to that power of God coming into the world in Jesus the Christ. They show that power at work, healing human ills. Yet these ills are very evidently still with us.

In the Anointing of the Sick, we do not expect physical miracles. This is so precisely because we are living in the post-resurrection times of Christ's Holy Spirit. So we look for the fruits of the Holy Spirit in those who receive this sacrament; we look for peace, for serenity before diminishment and death, for a new and different strength and for a sure and certain hope that God will fulfil his promises. So the fruits of the sacrament are internal, spiritual gifts that show Christ's victory over death by the fact that it can be approached in serenity, new strength and sure and certain hope. These gifts come from Christ's victory over death. The anointed sick are witnesses to his death and resurrection.

Chapter 7

Numbers at Mass

A CONCERNED PERSON might question what I have said so far by pointing to the falling numbers of people attending Mass. This is indeed a matter of concern.

From the beginning of this book, we have been working on the assumption that both the Church and Society are in a state of transition and that this transition is a crucial issue in understanding any aspect of our present time.

We are, as we have seen, no longer living in a society that breeds a sense of God's existence and importance in its members as had been the case in Western societies until the nineteenth and early twentieth centuries. This puts religious belief on a whole new footing. We have already seen that Stephen Bullivant puts it in his book *Mass Exodus*: 'If everyone shares the same beliefs, they are not beliefs, they are just how the world is'.[33]

Since the early twentieth century, Western European societies and their offshoots, such as Australia, have become

---

[33] S. Bullivant, *Mass Exodus. Catholic Disaffiliation in Britain and America since Vatican II.* OUP, 2019, p. 101.

more and more pluralised in their understanding of the world. These societies which were once formerly and professedly Christian, have now ceased being so in their social structures and ethos and have left the question of any religious affiliation as an open option for their individual members. This results in a great diversity of ways in which members of such societies understand how the world's and life's meaning is grounded. Some of these views are religiously based; others are not. Thus we now live in a new social context which does not provide any inner direction towards religiousness. And which has a tendency towards a relativism that finds worldviews hard to ground. Stephen Bullivant again suggests: 'The sheer presence of different worldviews side by side seems to weaken the taken for granted plausibility of each of them'.[34]

One of the characteristics of a society that is structurally Christian is that the external practices and structures tend to be emphasised over the internal dimensions of that faith. And once the external prompts, persuasions and regulations are removed, it lays bare either the depth or the shallowness of the internalisation of Christianity. This is true of any religiously structured society, whatever the religious tradition involved may be.

This gives rise to radical questions in a group that once took religious attitudes for granted and saw them as part of their inherited identity. Once the external scaffolding is removed, does the building stand or are people left wondering not only about what to believe but about whether

---

[34] Op.cit. p. 101.

to believe? I would suggest that there are those who feel freed up by the removal of the external restraints, others who decide to follow their own version of faith and others again who decide that there is no point to faith. This new situation can also provide the opportunity for a rediscovery of faith. But there will always be very significant consequences to this removal of religious social structures.

This change from a society in which the Christian faith was an integral part of the social, cultural and political scene to a society in which religion is to be an individual option for members of the society will inevitably make a difference to the numbers of people attending the celebration of the Eucharist. The significance of the Eucharist will no longer be obvious and taken for granted. Some people will not have a sufficient sense of either believing or belonging to make their being at the Eucharist a matter of importance.

A Church of concentric circles?

The Church at the present moment is rather like a series of untidy and intersecting concentric circles. At the centre of these concentric circles is that group which regularly gathers for the Sunday Eucharist. This centre is indispensable; it provides a point of reference for the whole untidy reality of Christian belonging.

There are many people who see themselves as Catholic for whom that core group is a point of reference to which they see themselves as belonging in loose, occasional and perhaps rather fuzzy ways. People who put themselves down as Catholic on a Census form often have no intention of regularly attending Sunday Mass; they may attend occasionally but those attendances are more likely to be about the occasion than about Sunday Mass. Such occasional attendance may involve the great feasts, funerals, baptisms, marriages, or occasions associated with their children's schooling. There can also be real attitudes of faith in people in such a situation. Other people may no longer see the Eucharist and the Church as a point of reference at all, but may still consider themselves Christian. The Spirit of God does indeed blow where it wills.

So what does it mean to be Catholic or Christian ? The many and varied stances of people who call themselves Catholic or Christian raises the above question. Many people continue to call themselves Christian and their basis for that is of their own devising or may depend on some inherited element of the faith to which they cling. Such elements can at times be stepping stones to a richer faith but can also result in positions which are in contrast or even opposition not only to what has been traditionally considered as making one a Christian, but also to the core reality which does make someone Christian.

The ultimate point of reference for being a Christian is the person of Jesus Christ. And we cannot simply reduce that reference to what suits us. In the final analysis, it has to be grounded directly or indirectly in the means by which we can know Jesus the Christ: the Scriptures and the tradition.

In saying this, we need to be aware that this tradition is never static. It is an ongoing way of life and is always in dialogue with the signs of the times[35] that is, with the different situations in which believers find themselves and seek to express their faith. This dialogue is always ongoing. And this is crucial to the understanding and handing on of the faith. There is a great saying attributed to the artist Pablo Picasso that tradition is not wearing your grandfather's hat but giving birth to a child.

This dialogue is a matter for the whole community of faith with their different capacities and ministries. It involves in a particular way the work of theologians whose especial task is to be a believer who seeks to understand their faith more deeply and systematically in the context of their times. In every age of transition, there have been divisions about what needs to be carried forward in the tradition and what belongs purely to the former context in which the faith was lived out.

In chapter one of this book, we saw that such a situation occurred in New Testament times as the Church moved out of the purely Jewish context of its origins into the new context of the world of the Greco-Roman Empire. And we also saw that such a transition occurred in the fourth and fifth centuries with the basic understanding of Christianity being re-expressed in the thought world of ancient Greece and Rome. This occurred in and around the first Ecumenical Councils which were seeking to give clearer expression to the mystery of Christ's person and to the mystery of the Trinity.

---

[35] *Gaudium et Spes*, nos 4, 11, 44.

As we also saw in the same chapter a similar transition is going on around us today as we seek to express the same faith in Christ in the new context of our times in order that it be made clear to people of today; and the need for such clarity is also crucial for us as believers.

Do we need to be initiated into the Eucharist?

Given what has been said above, how will people come to be part of the Church and its Eucharist? Above we spoke of the osmosis effect by which people absorbed their faith from living in a Christian society. But what happens when that Christian society no longer exists and there cannot be any such osmosis?

There has to be something which takes the place of the 'Christianising' society's capacity to make its members in its own likeness. This is a critical question for the Church today. There is a great deal of thought and action about evangelisation going on in the Church both at the official level of Church documents[36] and in theological and pastoral research and writing.[37] Evangelisation is about speaking of

---

[36] This has become a recurrent theme in magisterial documents. Two outstanding documents are *Evangelii Nuntiandi* (On Evangelisation in the Modern World) of Pope Paul VI, 1975 and *Evangelii Gaudium* (The Joy of the Gospel) of Pope Francis, 2013

[37] See for instance: M. Dumais, *After Emmaus. Biblical Models for the New Evangelisation.* Collegeville, Minnesota: Liturgical Press, 2014; C. Taylor, J. Casanova, G. F. McLean, J. J. Vila-Cha (eds), *Renewing the Church in a Secular Age.* Washington D.C.: The Council for Research in Values and Philosophy, 2016; R. F. Leavitt, *The Truth will make you free. The New Evangelisation for a Secular Age.* Collegeville, Minnesota: Liturgical Press Academic, 2019.

Christ and his good news effectively in the context of our new and different times.

There are similarities between the Christianity of the first three centuries and that of today. In those centuries, Christians were small groups of believers in the midst of a large society whose members were followers of many different religions. The Church in those centuries gradually created the catechumenate. This was a form of initiation into the Church by which those desiring to be Christians were formed in the knowledge of the mystery of Christ and all that was associated with it, and in the behaviour that flowed from it. This process took each individual member a number of years. It went through various stages and it reached its culmination in baptism, confirmation and the Eucharist celebrated at Easter as the feast of the Lord's resurrection.

Do we need some equivalent for out times? The introduction of the *Rite for the Christian Initiation of Adults* was a prophetic act of the post-Vatican II Church.[38] This presents an adaptable process by which adults can come to an appreciation of the Christian Faith. Many parishes in many different countries can attest to the effectiveness of this form of initiation.

Along with this there has been a great number of initiatives and programs especially since Vatican II which have sought to give people a deeper understanding of their faith.

---

[38] *Ordo Initiationis Christianae Adultorum*, Typis Polyglottis Vaticanis, 1972. This was translated into English as *Rite of Christian Initiation of Adults*. Sydney/Wellington: E. J. Dwyer, 1987.

Christianity needs a means of initiation. The establishment of a Christian society was the means of initiation into the Christian Faith over the centuries of an established Christian society which was there presenting the Faith to all and presuming their acceptance of it. The whole society immersed its members in the Christian Faith and required that they accept it.

There always has to be some form of initiation. People cannot simply become Christian without an introduction to it. Sometimes one hears it said that people ought to be able to go to Mass, for instance, and take in what it is all about but they do have to be introduced to it. Similarly, it is not realistic to think that we can just speak to people about the faith and they will take it up. This form of simplistic evangelism is not evangelisation.

It is a central necessity for the Church today to realise that the old form of initiation has definitively come to its end along with the established Christian society to which it belonged.

This is not just about using contemporary media. We have to realise that the message itself has to be attuned to our new situation and context as it had been re-attuned for new contexts in the course of its long history.[39] This is a process which requires time and serious intellectual and pastoral creativity and effort as was the case in earlier times of significant transition. Just doing what we have always done will not be effective.

---

[39] *Evangelii Gaudium* 41, also note the quotation from Pope John XXIII in footnote 45 of *Evangelii Gaudium*.

Chapter 8

The Paschal Mystery

AS WE CELEBRATE THE LITURGY, what is it that is going on between God and ourselves? What is embodied by the symbols we engage in?

What we do in the liturgy is all focused on the death and resurrection of Jesus. All the prayers of the liturgy end with a phrase like 'through Christ our Lord'. If we look at the texts of any of the sacraments, we will see that they are all centred on Christ's death and resurrection. If we look at any of the Eucharistic Prayers, we will see that they present themselves explicitly as being 'in memory' of his death and resurrection and as enabling the participants to share in that death and resurrection. In the celebration of the liturgy we are being drawn from life as we know it now through death into a sharing in the life of the risen Lord.

We refer to Christ's death and resurrection – and our sharing in it – as the Paschal Mystery. This term has its roots in the Exodus or Passover of the Old Testament. The word paschal comes from the Hebrew word *pasch* meaning passover. The Christian passover is the passover of Jesus from life and the world as we know it through death into life and the world raised out of death into God's future. The liturgy is drawing us into this 'passing-over'. This is not a passing into another world but a re-creating and enlivening of the world we live in now as it enters a new dimension – that of union with God. The risen Jesus is still the same Jesus who existed in his earthly life: he bears the marks of his passion in his risen self. He is the new creation brought about by God. As we have seen in an earlier chapter this is happening already – but not yet – in accord with the essentially unfinished character of the Christian faith.

Jesus' death was brought about by the evil that is present in our world. Those immediately involved in his death as recounted in the gospels – the crowd, the religious authorities, Pontius Pilate, Judas, his own disciples and so on – were not just themselves as individuals. They embodied forces always at work in our world, at work in them, at that time, as well as before them and after them. They embodied the injustice and careerism that is at work in Pilate; they embodied the capacity of religious people to enter into fatal compromises and to close themselves off from the working of God by putting other 'religious' values before God; they embodied the mob mentality which can be so fickle and has led to so much injustice and violence; and in Judas we see embodied the capacity for betrayal that is strong in human history. A slice of such forces for evil is present among all human beings in one way or another and they have the capacity to tempt people to live in accord with them, as even Jesus was tempted to do (Matthew 4:1-17; Luke 4:1-13; Mark 1:12-13).

These people were doing to Jesus what had been done to so many before him and after him. He took upon himself the effects of such human evils as the prophet Isaiah had prophesied: 'And yet ours were the sufferings he bore, ours the sorrows he carried. But we, we thought of him as one punished, struck by God and brought low. Yet he was pierced through for our faults, crushed for our sins. On him lies a punishment that brings us peace, and through his wounds we were healed' (Isaiah 53:4-6.).

Those who brought about the death of Jesus directly were representatives of the sin or evil that goes on among human beings in all times and places. It is these death-dealing forces that have been overcome by the Father's raising Jesus to life out of the death imposed upon him by those forces. The Father has already overcome those forces – but 'not yet'!

As we read the accounts of Jesus' suffering and death, we are not just reading about what happened then but about what is happening now and what has so frequently happened throughout human history. We are reading about Jesus' solidarity with all who suffer injustice and victimisation. In reading the accounts of Jesus' resurrection, we are reading about those forces being frustrated in their attempt to extinguish what opposes them – frustrated by the power of God to give life even in the face of death.

Sin and death are often paired in the Scriptures and in the liturgy, because both are seen as separation from God. God, the life-giver, is the opposite of death which seems to be the end life. In the resurrection, we see that God's life-giving is not extinguished even by death; God turns death into a passage into life. Sin is also separation from God. It is incompatible with the God who is the Holy One; it creates separation from the life-giving God.

The risen Lord Jesus is beyond death and has overcome sin and evil by suffering its consequences and passing through them into life beyond them. To enter into communion with him is to begin to pass beyond the realm of sin and death.

There is, therefore, an essential moral dimension to communion with Christ which requires of us that we let his new 'yeast' leaven the batch which is ourselves (1 Corinthians 5:6-8). We are called along the path of following Jesus. As we read the gospels, we constantly place ourselves before his words and actions and are ourselves invited into the encounters he has with those who appear in the texts of the gospels. In the gospels, we are being invited to enter into the attitudes and actions that are his. In this endeavour we are in constant need of entering into communion with him through his word and in the Eucharist and of receiving his Spirit anew. These points of communion are the antidotes to the influence of sinfulness within and around us.

The gift

All of our life is a gift. We human beings receive life. We acknowledge this in the Blessings prayed during the Presentation of the Gifts at Mass. It is gifts we have received that we present as we begin the Eucharist. We are not pretending to give gifts to God but to receive and accept them and to bless God for them in expectation of yet more gift to come: 'the bread of life' and 'the cup of eternal salvation'.

Being gift is true of the whole universe of which we are part: the universe is a gift which we are gradually learning to unwrap by the work of human minds and hands which themselves are gifts received.

As the liturgy of the Eucharist plays out, we are taking in hand the gifts we have been given and responding to those gifts in an act of thanksgiving (beginning of the Eucharistic Prayer) followed by an act of supplication (final part of the Eucharistic Prayer) that God may complete what he has begun. And we do this in memory of Christ's death and resurrection in which that future, that completion, is anticipated.

And then we come to receive communion with hands outstretched not to grasp but to receive, to be gifted yet again with life by the God who has made us for himself. It is all gift. The death of Jesus which we celebrate in the Eucharist is the total gift of himself to us and for us. It is a gift of love from the very heart of God.

The great bargain

The Fathers of the Church described what goes on between God and ourselves as the *admirabile commercium*, which means the wonderful bargain or the great deal. In the liturgy, there is an exchange going on between God and ourselves. We present ourselves to the Father through, with and in Jesus Christ, in the symbolic forms of bread and wine, we hand our God-given selves over to the Father as Jesus did and we begin to receive the gift of re-created life from him. We give what we have received in order to receive yet more, a 'more' that the mind cannot yet conceive and that the heart cannot yet desire.

Sacrifice

I think that in the above we have a way of speaking about the death of Jesus and the Eucharist which is more engaging than the often-used language of sacrifice. It expresses what sacrifice once expressed in a very different culture and context. Sacrifice was a natural fit in cultures which were intrinsically religious but is a very ambiguous term to use in the culture which we currently inhabit.[40]

Sacrifice etymologically means 'to make sacred' or 'to transfer something into the sphere of the sacred'. The 'wonderful exchange' which plays out in the Eucharist takes us into communion with the One who is Sacred, who is himself the Holy One.

The word 'holy' is significant. As you will have noticed, it is a highly significant word in all the Eucharistic Prayers. In each one of them the acclamation of the 'Holy, Holy...' prayed by the whole congregation, is a crucial hinge. It is the point to which the Preface of the Eucharistic Prayer leads. Then in each Eucharistic Prayer we ask the Father to send his Spirit upon the gifts 'to make holy' this bread and wine. That is to take them into the realm of the 'Holy'.

The Second Eucharistic Prayer prays: 'Make holy, therefore, these gifts, we pray, by sending down your Spirit upon them like the dewfall, so that they may become...'. The Third Eucharistic Prayer prays: 'Therefore, O Lord, we humbly implore you, by the same Spirit, graciously make holy these gifts... that they may become....'. The Fourth Eucharistic

---

[40] See L-M Chauvet, 'Sacrifice: an Ambiguous Concept in Christianity', in *Concilium* 2013, 4, pp. 13-24.

Prayer prays similarly: 'Therefore, O Lord, we pray, may this same Holy Spirit graciously sanctify these offerings...'

Holiness in the Scriptures is the specific characteristic of God. It describes the difference that is God, the otherness of God; it is that characteristic of God which makes human beings take off their shoes before him. And yet it is also used of those people and things which have such contact with God that they are affected by it. But this holiness is always God's. So when the Christians of the New Testament are described as saints (holy ones), that does not specifically describe their own personal goodness so much as the holiness of God left as a kind of shine on them from their contact with God.

Thus when we ask God to make the gifts of bread and wine holy, we are asking him that they may become our means of contact with him in Christ; that they may be taken into the realm of the holy, so that in and through them we may become holy, that is, in communion with God the Holy One. This is one of the earliest ways of talking about the transformation of the gifts in the Eucharist and it remains important in the current Eucharistic Prayers.

A secondary meaning of sacrifice is that of giving up something in the light of something more valuable or important. We use the term frequently in this sense today. It is, however, a derived meaning of the term with regard to its scriptural usage which we have seen above. This derived use does, however, link into the scriptural usage because in the discovery of the 'Holy One' there may need to be a choice made between the value of the 'Holy' by comparison to other things which involves going beyond those other things. This is part of the transformation which the discovery of the 'Holy' can bring about in human beings.

Chapter 9

The Eucharist is Pentecost

AFTER RECOUNTING THE ACTIONS AND WORDS OF JESUS at the Last Supper, each Eucharistic Prayer continues by remembering the various phases of his passover, that is, his suffering, death, descent into hell, resurrection, and ascension into glory. The phases of his passover are remembered in all the Eucharistic Prayers of both the Eastern and Western Churches; they do this in greater and lesser detail and in varying ways.

There is an exception to this remembering, however, which is the final element of Christ's passover – the sending of the Holy Spirit. It does not get an explicit mention in Eucharistic Prayers. However the prayer which follows the memorial prayer is taken up entirely with the gift of the Spirit. This prayer is the Epiclesis. It calls for the coming of the Holy Spirit.

This arrangement is significant. The reason for this seeming omission is that each Eucharist is an instance of that coming of the Holy Spirit. The other phases of Christ's passover have as their ultimate fruit the coming of the Spirit and so memorial is made of them as the very source of the Eucharist being celebrated at that time and in that place. Pentecost is not mentioned but is actuated. The Memorial prayer refers to what happened in the past but the Epiclesis is about what happens in the present.

It is in the celebration of the Eucharist that the Church which had been brought to birth with the coming of the Spirit at Pentecost is again given birth in the here and now. This is what is being expressed in the Epiclesis of each Eucharist. The Epiclesis is given greater emphasis in the understanding of the Eucharist of the Churches of the East than are the words of the Lord in the account of the Lord's Supper, because it is the Spirit who brings about Christ's gift of himself to us now in the Eucharist.

In the contemporary Roman liturgy, the Epiclesis has been divided into two parts: the first calling the Spirit to come upon the gifts that they may become the body and blood of Christ which comes before the account of the Lord's Supper (or the Consecration) and the second occurring after the account of the Lord's Supper and the Memorial prayer which prays for the coming of the Spirit upon the Church. We can see this clearly in the formulation of the second Eucharistic Prayer of the Roman Missal, which reads: 'Make holy, therefore, these gifts, we pray, by sending down your Spirit upon them like the dewfall'. Then after the account of the Lord's Supper, we have: 'Humbly we pray that, partaking of the body and blood of Christ, we may be gathered into one by the Holy Spirit'. This two part Epiclesis gives the impression that there are two actions of the Spirit, one over the gifts and one over the Church as it shares communion in that bread and cup.

The new Eucharistic Prayers of Roman liturgy composed after the Second Vatican Council drew the Epiclesis from the Eucharistic Prayers of the Eastern Church in which the Epiclesis was much more explicit than in the present First Eucharistic Prayer of the Roman liturgy which had been the only Eucharistic Prayer in use in the Roman Rite before Vatican II.

However in the Eastern tradition, there is only one Epiclesis over gifts and the Church after the account of the Lord's Supper. The one Epiclesis of the Eastern Liturgies expresses more clearly the richer and more traditional idea that the Spirit makes of this bread and wine the means by which the participants become the Church. The Church in celebrating the Eucharist is becoming the Church in that very action, and can do so only by the power of the Spirit.

The split in the Epiclesis occurred because the Roman liturgy was underdeveloped in its expression of the action of the Holy Spirit in the Church and in the liturgy. The Roman Eucharistic Prayer (Eucharistic Prayer I) prayed a prayer for the acceptance of the offering being made both before and after the account of the Lord's Supper. So in composing the new Eucharistic prayers after the Second Vatican Council, the Epiclesis was split into two parts following the two part structure of the Roman Canon in its prayer for the acceptance of the gifts.

There was another reason for this and that was that the understanding of the presence of Christ in the bread and wine of the Eucharist had taken a different path in the Church of the West to that of the East. The composers of the new prayers wished to respect the path that the Western Church had taken.

This brings us to one of the most important things for enriching our understanding of the Eucharist. The Eucharist is an action of the Holy Spirit who at Pentecost made the Church the Church. That same Spirit continues to do that at each celebration of the Eucharist. The Holy Spirit is not an added extra to the life of the Church and the sacraments. They only come about by means of the action of the Holy Spirit. The Spirit sent to us by Christ creates our communion with Christ now.

In Western theology, we have tended to see the Eucharist as Jesus doing now what he did at the Last Supper. And, in so far as it goes, that is right. But because until recently our theology of the Holy Spirit had been somewhat neglected, this understanding of Christ's action was truncated because it tended to leave in obscurity the reality that what he does he does by means of his Spirit. This lack had led to earlier theological disputes about the meaning of memorial and how what happened 'then' can be effective 'now'.

The Eucharist, like all things Christian, is Trinitarian: 'Through Him (Christ), with Him and in Him, in the unity of the Holy Spirit, all glory and honour is yours, Almighty Father, forever and ever'. And we could put alongside 'in the unity of the Holy Spirit' other phrases like 'in the power of the Holy Spirit' or 'enabled by the Holy Spirit'.

In the Eucharist, we come before the Father through, with and in Christ who handed himself over to the Father in his life and death and who in his resurrection entered into the glory of the Father. We can enter into his passover because the Holy Spirit has united us to Christ in the communion celebrated in the Eucharist. We become caught up into the movement of Jesus to the Father which was his death and resurrection and so become participants in that death and resurrection.

This deepens our understanding of that patristic saying we have previously referred to: The Church makes the Eucharist and the Eucharist makes the Church.

The word and the Spirit

What has been said here about the Holy Spirit's action in the Eucharist is paralleled by that same Spirit's action in the proclamation and hearing of the word of God.

Earlier, we spoke of the text of the Scriptures read during the liturgy as being a sign of the word of God speaking his word to us now. Proclaiming the word is also sacramental. The word of God is handed on to us in the long biblical tradition in the words of human beings. The words of Scripture which we listen to as we gather for the liturgy of the Word are meant to find a home in us. As that word finds a home in us the word of God gets incarnated again in the minds and hearts of human beings. It is in this interplay between the word proclaimed and the word which enters into us now and which we take to heart, that the Holy Spirit is at work. It is that Spirit who is incarnating that word in us now as he incarnated the Word of God in the womb of Mary by his overshadowing of her.

Mary is our model in hearing that word. She was deeply disturbed by the words spoken to her and pondered what they might mean; she became afraid at hearing these words; she has questions about how this can be since she has no husband. She is promised the Spirit to enable what she is asked to do; she comes to say: 'Here I am, the Lord's servant, let it happen to me as you have said' (Luke 1:26-38). Mary goes through a whole process of hearing and accepting the word on her way to saying 'yes'. So it is with us as we hear the word of God spoken to us.

Consequences for the celebration of the liturgy

The awareness that the Eucharist involves the Coming of the Holy Spirit upon the Church has significant consequences for the celebration of the Eucharist. They are consequences which require a change of mentality in the approach to the celebration. The over-concentration of our liturgical awareness on the Consecration or the Account of the Last Supper in the Eucharistic Prayer has so diluted our appreciation and celebration of the rest of that prayer that something as important as the action of the Holy Spirit has fallen into shadow.

The whole purpose and meaning of the Eucharistic Prayer – and of the Eucharist as a whole – is that we are taken up into the action of Christ's handing over of himself to the Father. It does not call us to fall down in adoration so much as to stand up in the awareness of our communion with Christ in his passover into the Father's hands. This can only be by means of the presence and power of Christ's Spirit.

To limit the Eucharist to the presence of Christ in and through the consecrated bread and wine is to truncate its real significance, its full and proper reality. It is to cut the

Eucharistic action in half. The purpose of the Eucharist is to make of us a communion with Jesus Christ in his action on the cross and in his being raised to new life.

The Spirit and the liturgy

One of the clear implications of the Eucharist being a renewal of Pentecost is the importance of unity and universality. Those who received the Spirit at Pentecost received that Spirit as a group gathered in unity; all of them and each one received the Spirit.

In the Pentecost narrative, those who heard the words of that group who had received the Spirit heard them in their own many languages. As Luke graphically puts it in the Acts of the Apostles: 'Surely all these men speaking are Galileans? How does it happen that each of us hears them in his own native language? Parthians, Medes and Elamites, people from Mesopotamia, Judea and Cappadocia, Pontus and Asia, Phrygia and Pamphylia, Egypt and the parts of Libya round Cyrene, as well as visitors from Rome – Jews and proselytes alike – Cretans and Arabs; we hear them preaching in our own language about the marvels of God' (Acts 2:1-11). Their words gathered all these people into one.

Some biblical scholars also see a contrasting echo of the story of the Tower of Babel in the Pentecost account. Babel is the story of the dividing of humankind by the variety of its languages. Pentecost is the gathering of the peoples despite their differences of language. The liturgy certainly makes the connection between Pentecost and Babel by making the account of Babel the first reading of the Vigil Mass of the feast.

The nature of the Church involves dialogue. Dialogue is not just a matter of giving everyone their voice; it is a question of our fidelity to the Holy Spirit. In the Acts of the Apostles, when the apostles and elders send out their letter after their meeting in Jerusalem concerning the critical question of the Gentiles becoming Christians (Acts 15), they declare that their resolution 'has been decided by the Holy Spirit and by ourselves....' (v. 28). Their decision came about not by any individual claiming to have the right answer but by communal discussion and discernment. One could say by a dialogue that opened the way for the influence of the Holy Spirit. Perhaps effective celebrations of the liturgy require preparation that takes such dialogue into account.

A third crucial point for the spiritual functioning of the Church is the recognition of gifts and ministries. To block such gifts from finding expression in the life of the Church is also to block the working of the Spirit in the Church. As St Paul puts it in his first letter to the Corinthians: 'There are varieties of gifts, but the same Spirit; and there are varieties of services, but the same Lord. There are varieties of activities but the same God who activates all of them in everyone. To each person the manifestation of the Spirit is given for the general good.' (1 Corinthians 12: 4-7).

We need to capitalise on the awareness that the liturgy is fruitful because the Spirit is at work within the Church and its liturgy. The liturgy is not automatically fruitful; it is fruitful by means of the interplay between Christ and his people which takes place in the power of the Holy Spirit. The liturgy requires participation.

Chapter 10
'For you and for all'

UNDERLYING ALL THAT HAS BEEN PROPOSED so far in this book is a way of looking at the Church which is crucial to the Church's path into the future and crucial to its credibility.

This renewed understanding of the Church is, of course, grounded in the Second Vatican Council which functions as a watershed between the past and the future and as the formal ecclesial inspiration for the age into which we are moving. Vatican II does not have an immediate answer to all of our contemporary questions but it sowed the seeds whose flowering will lead us into the future. That Council can claim to echo the words of the apostolic letter in the Acts of the Apostles: 'It has been decided by the Holy Spirit and by ourselves...' (Acts 15:28). It can claim to be such an echo in a way that no other body can. It is our major point of reference as we move into this new age of the Church. There is a parallel between those who do not accept Vatican II and those who sought to avoid accepting the apostolic letter of the Acts of the Apostles.

No Ecumenical Council has ever laid out so extraordinary an understanding of the Church as did the Second Council of the Vatican. And it did this in its two major ecclesial documents: the Document on the Church (*Lumen Gentium*) and the Document on the Church in the Contemporary World (*Gaudium et Spes*). In other documents, it treated matters closely aligned with the above documents, especially notable the document on Divine Revelation (*Dei Verbum*), that on Missionary Activity (*Ad Gentes*) and that on Religious Liberty (*Dignitatis Humanae*). And an understanding of the Church permeates the Document on the Sacred liturgy (*Sacrosanctum Concilium*) as I hope to have shown throughout this book.

In the first paragraph of the first chapter of the Document on the Church, we find the following statement which underlies the rest of the document and indeed all the work of the Council:

> By her relationship with Christ, the Church is a kind of sacrament or sign of intimate union with God and the unity of all mankind (*sic*); she is also an instrument for the achievement of such union and unity.

It is significant that this statement appears in the first chapter of the document whose title is 'The Mystery of the Church'. As we have seen earlier, the word 'Mystery' – when used in theology and liturgy – refers to human realities in which the divine can be discovered. So, for example, we speak of the Mystery of Christ, or of the Church or of the Eucharist.

Such things have this character precisely as realities of our human world. In their very humanness they are mysteries. The Church remains utterly human with all that is good and ill that is part of that humanity. But even as such it remains a place where the divine can be discovered; the Holy One can be discovered within it. It is for this reason only that such a statement as made in the Creed can make sense: 'I believe in the holy catholic Church'.

This understanding of the Church elaborated by Vatican II is deliberately put forward over against an earlier understanding which can be epitomised in the adage 'Outside the Church there is no salvation' (*Extra Ecclesiam nulla salus*). In this understanding, the Church was seen as the only way of salvation, so if you were outside the Church you could not be saved or at least your salvation was at risk.

In the course of the twentieth century, such an understanding had been considerably modified not only among the people and among theologians but also in statements of the Magisterium of the Church as is evidenced in the case of the American Fr Feeney who was condemned by the Holy Office for proposing a strict interpretation of the above adage, that is, that no one outside the Catholic Church could be saved.[41]

Such an interpretation is not only theologically unacceptable but contradicts the common sense faith of the Catholic people. It became unbelievable and unacceptable.

---

[41] The Letter of the Holy Office to the Archbishop of Boston. 8 August 1949 *Denzinger-Schonmetzer* 3866-3873. See F. A. Sullivan, *Salvation outside the Church?* Mahwah NJ: Paulist Press, 1992.

In place of this earlier understanding of the purpose of the Church, we have this renewed understanding based on a view of the Church as the sacrament or sign of the salvation of all humankind.

What is meant by this?

As we have seen, sacraments or signs point beyond themselves to another reality, to something which we cannot see with our eyes or touch with our hands. So the Eucharist is a sacrament because it takes us beyond its sign dimension to something else which is not visible or tangible. It draws us into communion with the Risen Lord. It is so with each of the sacraments in its own way.

Similarly, the Church is a sign or sacrament of union with God and of unity among human beings. This is the union and unity which God, through Christ, is seeking to bring about in his future kingdom. Now he raises up the Church as an image of that future union and unity. The Church in its own frail way is a sign of what is to come.

We can compare this to an iceberg. The Church is that part of the iceberg that is above the waters while the greater part of the iceberg is below the waters. God's activity in the Church is like that part of the ice which is above the water but so much more of God's activity is going on at a level we cannot see. And just as we can only know that ice is submerged below the waters by seeing the ice above the waters, so we come to know God's activity in all the world, because of its sign that is the Church, the community of believers.

The Church is essentially a part of God's activity in the world; it does not have its own identity apart from that world which God is seeking to bring to himself. The former way of understanding the Church summed up in 'Outside the Church no salvation' tends to see the Church as something existing for itself and as over and above the world, as self-sufficient. The vision of the Church based in Vatican II sees the Church as essentially part of the world, as having its purpose in its very relationship to the world. The Church is that group of human beings which has come to know of God's saving plan; they exist as a promise for all.

Relationship with Christ

None of the above can make sense without the first phrase of the above quotation from the Document on the Church: 'By her relationship with Christ, the Church...'.

The specific character of the Church's relationship with Christ is that it is explicit and reciprocal. Christ is present to all of creation but that relationship becomes explicit and reciprocal in the community of believers, the Church. The ultimate basis of that explicitness and reciprocity is in the earthly life of Jesus during which he gathers disciples around himself. This brings about a new relationship between those human beings and God in and through Jesus the Christ. This relationship is parallel to any other relationship which can only develop when it becomes explicit and reciprocal.

This relationship continues differently in the Church after the historical life of Jesus by means particularly of the Scriptures and the Breaking of the Bread. In fact, by means of those things – we have already mentioned – which Christians are called to be faithful to in the Acts of the Apostles 2:42:

'the teaching of the apostles, the fellowship, the breaking of the bread and the prayers'. By those means, relationship with the Risen Lord continues. It continues in these new forms. Even though Christ's presence is mediated in these forms, it remains explicit and reciprocal through them. It is thus that Jesus the Christ can be known and followed in a way that gives an echo of his presence in our world.

Christians are simply human beings like all others. They have everything in them which is in all other human beings – of good and of ill. What is specific to them is their relationship with Christ, the fact that they are Christ-ian. They are human beings who are called to live in dialogue with the words of Christ, the actions of Christ and especially with his death and resurrection.

The first fruits

There is another image with which to describe the purpose of the Church which can be drawn from the Scriptures. This is the image of the first fruits of the harvest.

The biblical rite of the first fruits was a rite in which the first fruits of the harvest and the firstlings of the flock were offered to God in place of the whole crop or the whole flock. *They were the part which stood in for the whole.*

The first fruits were offered in recognition that God was the source of nature and its fruitfulness, in recognition that the whole harvest and indeed the whole of creation comes from God and belongs to God. The first fruits were offered in recognition of the One who kept human beings alive through the gifts of creation and so it was also an offering of thanksgiving. The first fruits were given over to God, offered to God because the whole harvest came from God and belonged to God. By this means the whole harvest was recognised as holy and at the same time was given over to human use. *The first fruits make sense only in relation to the whole harvest.*

The New Testament usage

The New Testament uses this term 'first fruits' figuratively and its use is very valuable in enabling us to give expression to the meaning of the Church and its relationship to humankind, and indeed to the whole of creation. This in turn only makes sense because of the relationship of the Church to Christ.

We find several uses of this term in the New Testament and mainly in the Pauline writings. First, in 1 Corinthians 15:20 and 22-23, Christ is described as 'the first fruits of those who have fallen asleep' (v. 20) and then we find 'For as in Adam all die so also in Christ shall all be made alive. But each in his own order: Christ the first fruits, then at his coming those who belong to Christ' (vv. 22-23). So Christ in his resurrection is the first fruits of the new harvest which harvest involves all who belong to Christ. Already we are raised in him the first fruits and yet – we are not!

Secondly, in Romans 8:23, those gathered to Christ are described as having the first fruits of the Spirit who groans inwardly as they await the resurrection of their bodies. This is related to the groaning of all creation as it is in travail, seeking its liberation and true birth. Those who have the first fruits of the Spirit – those who belong to Christ – are related by that fact to the whole of creation and to the future of which the Spirit is the first fruits. Having the first fruits of the Spirit makes of Christians the first fruits of all creation.

Then in Romans 11:16, those Jews who have become members of Christ are described as the first fruits of the whole of Israel. The relationship of the Jews who have accepted Christ to the rest of the Jewish people is seen in the image of the first fruits.

Then there are two telling applications of this metaphor to people who have become Christians. In Romans 16:5, we find Paul speaking of Epanaetus, who is the first fruits of Asia for Christ. Paul sees Epanaetus' conversion to Christ in the image of the first fruits. He does not see him just as an individual who has been converted but he is Asia in so far as he is Asia's first fruits. In him, Asia has already come to Christ but – not yet!

We have the same metaphor used of Stephanas' family in 1 Corinthians 16:15. This family is described by Paul as the first fruits of Achaia for Christ; in them, Achaia has already come to Christ but – not yet!

Going beyond the Pauline literature, we find this usage in the letter of James 1:18: 'By his own choice he gave birth to us by the message of the truth so that we should be a sort of first fruits of all his creation'. In this passage, James sees the relationship of Christians to the whole of God's creation in the image of the first fruits.

The Book of Revelation 14:4 likewise uses the image in describing the one hundred and forty-four thousand redeemed followers of the Lamb as first fruits. They are described as having 'been redeemed from humankind as first fruits for God and the Lamb'. This one hundred and forty-four thousand are not the only ones saved. They are the first fruits of the whole.

Theology

These passages provide us with an image that can be developed theologically as a way to conceive the identity and the purpose of the Church in its inherent relationship to all humankind and all of creation.

Such a relationship between the Church and Humankind is only possible because those who make up the Church are called to reflect the light of Christ who is in himself the light of the nations.[42]

Christ is the first fruits. In the dead and risen Christ, humankind and all of creation has come to the fulfilment of God's intentions for it. In him, the future has occurred and has come into the present. From him, the new life and the renewal of creation comes to us. In him, redemption and new life are already achieved; in the rest of us, they are not yet achieved as we are in the process of passing over from death to life and from sin to holiness.

We use the image of the first fruits to speak of the Church, the communion of Christ's disciples, only because of that very communion with Christ by which his gifts are already at work among human beings in seed if not in full flower. The Church is but the moon to Christ's sun – to use an image

---

[42] *Lumen Gentium.* 1.

dear to many of the Fathers of the Church. Whatever the Church has got to offer comes not from itself but solely from Christ.

The Church as first fruits

In the image of the first fruits, you cannot separate the first fruits from the whole harvest. The first fruits are of their very nature part of and related to the whole harvest or the whole flock. They contain and re-present the whole. The harvest and the first fruits are essential to each other.

If we look at the Church through this metaphor, the link between the Church – those gathered around Jesus Christ – and the rest of humankind is of the Church's essence. It is a primary element in understanding the Church. *The Church can make no sense without that relationship.* And in terms of God's plan in Christ, the Church is of crucial historical importance to humankind.

In those human beings who by their union with Christ make up the Church, we have the first fruits of God's ultimate gathering of all humankind to himself. This group, the People of God, is about the future of humankind in God's plan not about themselves as a group taken out of humankind. It is not a sect. This group of human beings provide the image of that future which they prefigure and bring into the process of human history by their presence within that history. The Church is the symbol or sacrament of humankind in its relationship to God in Christ. The Church is humankind caught up consciously in the passover of Christ into God.

Without the first fruits, the whole cannot know or achieve its ultimate end and, without the whole, the first fruits loses its reason for being. God's plan is primarily about the redemption or making new of humankind, indeed of the whole creation. The Church is a sign and instrument of that plan. It does not exhaust that plan but is its sign and instrument.

Representative function

Just as Christ has a representative function with regard to all humankind – he is the Son of Man, the representative human being from the point of view embedded in God's plan – so those gathered around Christ – his People – likewise take on a representative function in relation to all humankind. They come before the Father in Christ and in the Spirit as the first fruits of all humanity, if you like as humanity, now enabled to do this.

It is in the name of all that this People gives thanks and praise, intercedes and offers themselves for union with Christ. As the Fourth Eucharistic Prayer prays before the Sanctus: 'United with them (the hosts of heaven) and in the name of every creature under heaven, we too praise your glory as we say: Holy...'. And as the same Prayer prays in the Intercessions: 'Remember those who take part in this offering, those here present, all your people and all who seek you with a sincere heart'.

The Church's mission is about bringing people to Christ. This can involve conversion to Christ but it always involves standing before God in and with Christ as the first fruits of the future, as the representatives of all, as the sacrament of humankind. And in so doing, bringing the whole of creation before God in Christ. In this we are called to rejoice in our humanity in all its extraordinary richness and to repent of the evil with which we and humanity are burdened.

The mission we have will never be achieved until all of humankind is gathered at the table of the Father as the body of the glorified Lord. That day will come at God's doing. For now we are the servants of a Mystery beyond us whose fulfilment we long for and pray for. We are servants of a Mystery, a kingdom, whose signs in human history we look out for in order to work for its coming. We are, in other words, a priestly, prophetic and serving people.

The eschatological tension

The image of the first fruits emphasises well that essential dimension of the Church's life which we call the eschatological tension, which has been discussed in chapter six of this book. This is the tension between what is achieved already for all humankind in Christ and the final flourishing of that achievement at Christ's coming. At the Easter Vigil, we don't just celebrate the resurrection of Christ, we celebrate the resurrection in expectation of his coming. It is a night of vigil, of waiting for the Lord. We are 'like men waiting for their master's return so that when he arrives he will find them wide awake and will seat them at his table'.[43]

We are redeemed and we are not yet redeemed! We still die and the ravages of evil are only too visible around us.

---

[43] *Roman Missal*, Easter Vigil, no. 1.

This tension is of the essence of Christianity. The Christian is caught in this tension and lives in it. We live in incompleteness and the burden of human sinfulness weighs upon us and our world. This needs to be built into our understanding of the Church and the practice of Christian life. There can be no pretense of perfection or completeness in spirit or morality or structure. Nothing is as yet completely penetrated by the Kingdom of God or the Spirit of Christ. We are all caught up in human ambiguity and within that we are called to take up Christ's call to conversion, to that *metanoia*, that call of his to us to go beyond ourselves and the way we are now, in mind, heart and action. We live in this tension in the knowledge that it will never be resolved until the master's return.

Christians: 'a cognitive minority'

We need to place this discourse on the Church as the first fruits of humankind in the much more complex context of a pluralist world. In terms of religious traditions and worldviews, the Christian tradition is one among many. Each tradition or worldview has its particular view of the world and humankind arising out of its particular character and none of these is the same.

Yves Congar uses the term 'cognitive minority' as a way of describing what we mean when we speak of the Church as the 'first fruits' in the pluralist situation of many ways of approaching the world.[44] Cognitive minorities are groups

---

[44] Y. Congar, *La parole et le soufflé. Nouvelle Edition augmentée de la lecture de Remi Cheno*. Paris: Mame-Desclee, 2010, p. 200.

within a society which have specialist or particular knowledge about some aspect of our common human reality which it is their responsibility to make explicit, maintain and promote. For instance, there are those involved in medicine, those engaged in the arts, those charged with political responsibility, each of these groups has specialist knowledge and practical expertise which is not possessed by the whole society. Yet these particular groups exist in relation to the rest of society and for its sake; they serve the whole in terms of their area of specialty.

In highly complex societies such as most contemporary societies, this differentiation and specialisation is both inevitable and important. Without such groups a particular area of expertise would be missing from ongoing human history and endeavour.

The Church as the first fruits is like one of these cognitive minorities. It has a particular point to make which cannot be made without it. Unless this group is there to speak of Christ and embody him in human history, his importance remains dormant and ineffective in ongoing human history.

Those who are part of that communion with Christ called the Church make a unique claim about that same Christ. They claim that he is of absolute importance not just for them but for the whole human race and for all of creation. We proclaim that in him humanity will find its ultimate end and purpose and in him it will find the One from whom it comes. In him God is incarnate; in him God is en-histored! This is part of the particularity of the Christian claim which other parallel groups do not make. This is our particular discovery about the world.

This ought not to inhibit us from recognising the particular claims of other traditions. The very fact that these claims are in fact different to each other enables each one to respect the others and ought to facilitate dialogue between them. Dialogue is an essential dimension of the future. We only claim one field of expertise and that is the knowing of Christ Jesus, which nothing can outweigh (Philippians 3:8).

Conclusion

In conclusion, I would like to quote a passage from Pope Francis' letter on evangelisation: 'Pastoral ministry in the missionary key seeks to abandon the complacent attitude that says "We have always done it this way".'[45]

This is critically true for the liturgy and liturgical ministry. We need to look seriously at our practice and this is especially true for those of us who are ordained ministers.

This re-assessing of our liturgy must be guided by the two great thrusts of Vatican II and its liturgical reform: fidelity to tradition and adaptation to the contemporary context, named *aggiornamento* by Pope John XXIII.[46]

Throughout this book, there has been an attempt to look at the liturgy and especially the Mass in accord with these two thrusts. What is presented does not pretend to be the last word but to be a stimulus to further thought and renewed practice.

We can never abandon our long, beautiful and historically-shaped tradition nor can we ever ignore the inadequacies

---

[45] *Evangelii Gaudium*, no. 33.
[46] GIRM, nos 2-15.

which make that tradition hard to communicate or even incommunicable in our present context. The history of the Catholic tradition is one of continuity in change. This can be seen in the great turning points like that of the first century movement out of Judaism into the Roman world or that of the fourth century reformulation of the tradition of faith for a new cultural context.

We cannot ignore the fact that the liturgy has little purchase on many of our contemporaries in our pluralist and secular cultures. This calls for much considered attention and serious creativity.

As I hope is clear from this book, we are not just dealing with a liturgical matter in the narrow sense of the word. Liturgy is not an isolated part of the Church's life distinct from all the other strands of that life. It is not mere ritual! It is where we become who we are! It celebrates and communicates the whole mystery of Christ among us. And so all the areas of theological reflection are drawn into it.

The liturgy does not have guaranteed fruitfulness. It is given to us as our means of communion with Jesus Christ. Its fruitfulness comes about in a covenantal fashion, that is by the conjoining of the liturgical action and those celebrating it. That is the reason that the participation of all is seen as the aim to be achieved above all else in the renewal of the liturgy. The presence of Christ is given to us but the fruitfulness of that presence comes about by the interplay of his gift and the celebrating people. So the human actions asked of us by the liturgy are crucial.

The liturgy follows the pattern of the covenant. Marriage is the great image of the covenant in the Scriptures and the working of the liturgy can be understood well in that same image. Marriage is fruitful by means of the openness and self-giving of the two partners. So it is with the liturgy: it is by means of our openness and self-giving in the liturgy that the presence of God among us in Christ can become fruitful in us.

I hope that this book may be some help in the ongoing process of the renewal and *aggiornamento* of the Church and of the liturgy.

The Lord be with us all!

www.ingramcontent.com/pod-product-compliance
Lightning Source LLC
Chambersburg PA
CBHW010707020526
44107CB00082B/2703